Ex libris

Yolanda Lilyan Brown

THE MASTER H

THE MASTER

H

BY

PENSATIA

THE EUCLID PRESS • NEW YORK 1961

By the same author

"A JOURNEY INTO THE LIGHT"

NOTE

Pensatia is a symbolic name given to Helen Merrick Bond, under which she was directed to write, when chosen to record this Teaching from the Master H.

During a long membership in the Rosicrucian Order, Mrs. Bond has cultivated the strength and poise so vital to all students and seekers of the Way. Always inspired to pursue a path of service . . . the amanuensis has again dipped her pen . . . and recorded the message "as revealed" upon her many Spiritual Sojourns with the Master.

CONTENTS

THE MASTER H

PRELUDE

I walked far within, to that infinite quiet. There on fourth dimensional hill of green my Spiritual Guide and Teacher came and bade me write The Master H. *I Pensatia, do obey. God give me health and wisdom to hear the Master's words.*

PENSATIA

Dedicated to my brothers Richard and Charles

"Think not, O neophyte, or seeker at the Gate of Life, that a Master, or Masters, spring full-bloomed from life's wheel. Aye, many lives, many sucklings from a mother's breast, many bouts with earth; aye, many loves, sorrows and dark nights brew the magic crucible which brings forth the Master.

"Remember, from a Cain's past often lies the seed of tomorrow's Master, and from a Satan's sorrow is conceived the 'White Servant' of our Lord. It is written in the Hall of Wisdom: Many colors, all experiences, mistake after mistake is the Holy Mating which makes a Master live.

"O Holy Sacred Path where all the Masters trod and do! It is in the vitals of life, in the Alpha and Omega that one's cry for Mastership comes forth. In the world's young dawn, in the borning of all souls, God the Father proclaimed all may become Masters, if they so choose.

"Yet ever is the question asked: 'Why so few Masters?' Why indeed? O shame to Light, Life and Love, to Humanity, shame to ignorance and to Maya's lure, yet compassion and forbearance to the human race. 'Why?' you ask. It is a healthy question and calls forth an honest answer. This is it in relative degree . . .

"The fiat of the Creator is: All souls born in womb of matter, though equal to choose, and free, do declare by their choice their path for or against Mastership. It is true that in many or less incarnations, all will take the Master Road. Yet individually each must make the decision. A shepherd among the valleys green, a taxi driver among busy cities, a farmer of the soil, those of royal blood, or one with coined gold and silver—all can and may heed the call to Mastership. Alas—so few heed the inner voice, so few, that it seems a rarity.

"Mastership is a call, a seed in all, implanted by Cosmic Father. Man himself must sprout and bring forth its infallible mantle. Those who brave the initiations of fire, water, air and earth are the way showers, the Teachers of humanity's march to the Heaven within. They are the Magi—the Xmas Star personified, the Great Illuminati from Isis' Heart. They walk the earth in humble guise and still man's stormy waters—they point the Way, for they have trod the Way and won. They are love, warm understanding, forgiving. For did not the Father give all to them, even as He does to all who obey and take the Master Path?

"What is a Master? A Master is he or she, or they, who dare to pierce the veil of ignorance, who dare beyond Maya's illusions, who valiantly walk within and up in consciousness to attain the White Light, who immortally live on earth as in Heaven. A Master is he who is crowned Humanity's Prince and Heaven's Son . . . one who has drank from all waters of life and donned all colors, one who has died and risen with cosmic consciousness his privilege, right, his Word of power. A Master is he who knows —he who speaks and works with Life's Cosmic Plan. He is the pioneer in cosmic realms, one who earns the right to bring to earth diamonds of the soul and plant them in loam of matter. They are the transmuters, the Alchemists who make gold—give gold, and are gold, shining, everlasting. A Master is he who wears the Christ imprint between his eyes, that signature of Light that shines forever out to man.

"Masters must be, else the earth slip back into the dross of pagan yesterdays. Masters ever whisper in the heart of man God's eternal song. They ignite, they stir for man knowledge of this age-old Path of the Masters. Thus it is, I Master H write through Pensatia, she who is a student and hears my words and thus obeys. All God's strength be given her to write this History of Mastership.

"Be it known—to her and others, they who come under my tutorship—I first saw the light of day in a green and fertile valley back in Chaldea, back where a river flowed

beside my native tent. I remember my first earth mother—
that is, my first life memory (before that, all was blank)—
yes, my ardent recollection was mother, lean, young and
most noble of eye, and the winds softly mingling with her
gentle lullaby. I ran, played, grew lusty and walked the
pleasant desert and valley earth with my bearded father.
Aye, I was rich, for he taught me to look up to the stars and
learn, and trained me to hear the sound of earth, air and
stream. I was schooled in hardships, yet with wisdom of
the heart my mother spoke of God. And young, I heard
and obeyed the call to Mastership. That is, in the dawn of
my many incarnations, I heard the 'Sacred Call'—that I
did digress many times—O reader, you will learn. Yet on
that first round of earth life remembered, I did sip deeply
at the foundation of Mastership—it was grounded in blood
and bone. I grew tall and sturdy as trees of the forest. I met
and loved She who to this day and into Heaven is my complement in woman. Like the merry ripple of the wind, still
is heard the music of her name. Though through her on
my Path of Mastership came my first impact with sorrow.
O vainglorious youth! . . . to think I would be spared the
common cup of mankind . . . the parting of those we love.
Yet, had I then learned that in reality there is no parting,
that love is never lost, how much sooner would I have obtained Mastership. Let it be known, the first and last law
learned on the Master Path is that there is no death, that
love once given is forever. Yet when my beloved donned
the robe of transition, I threw away my tools of Mastership—aye, I threw away my parental habitat, I tore asunder all that spoke of the Rose, the Lotus. I vowed to
live as earthlings live, no more, no less. In pain and sorrow
I grayed my parents' hair with my wanton indifference.
And when a caravan, journeying to distant land arrived, I
severed my natal ties, traveled, and made port at the Isle
of Samos. And there I did meet my Guru in my thirtieth
year. I was felled by a great fever. In my delirium I was

conscious of the tall, dark-bearded Master keeping vigil at my side. When the crisis was past, he it was who ever after *led* me to the Holy Grail.

"Let it be known—even then as now, 'When the student is ready the Master appears.' Only when lightning strikes in the human heart, when a darkness blights living and all held values, perchance, the gate opens and causes generate the Master's approach. So it was on the Isle of Samos, my early foundation—even though I had sought to discard all. Yet hear this vital truth: that which is ingrained lives forever even though ignored for many lives; that which is started is destined to grow. So past causes and effects drew me to Samos and my Guru.

"There by study, practice and the beloved aid of my Master, I passed in one incarnation the initiations of earth, fire, air and water. Then one silent evening hour, in the sacred grove of Samos, my Guru gave me the ancient salutation of Rose and Cross, and bade me leave and be on my own, and travel until I made the illuminated Light of Mastership.

"Many lives passed. I reincarnated in the Black race, the Jewish, in Spain, in Egypt. I was known as 'the Athenian' of old Greece. England, and the warm blood of Italy cradled my births. Yes, I—as all—traversed the Wheel of Life. Now all is one—each link . . . holy ground weaving the high consciousness of my soul out to life.

"I Master H live now to give, to serve and to aid my disciples to find the Holy Grail, the Alchemical Rose and the Elixir of Everlasting Life. My disciples know me at first as an overshadowing presence, or a feeling of love when working at their alchemical toil. A few will see me in flesh. Yet know that is not important. If by grace, or if one's mission warrants such, I make possible this interlude with myself. Yet all contacts with me are true, in heart or conscious awareness. I make myself known when the student is ready. Or when, as I now write through you,

Pensatia, as you reach in clear awareness the green hills of the Cosmic. Here, I come and relate to you the History of a Master.

"Remember, all are potential Master timber. All in some Wheel of Life must and will take the Master Path. Remember also, every act, thought—outgoing, constructive, creative—is a star leading one to the Master, consciously or unconsciously. Yes, all peoples of earth, none can escape their final destiny—Yoga, Union with God.

"As in life, Mastership is earned by degrees, by experience, by practice in all the arts of living. A disciple is tested and tried until he bends, but never breaks with the waves and storms of Maya. At every crest of discipleship, honors and recognition from within and from without are bestowed upon the true disciple. Even though all worldly gains for the moment might be taken away—for it is the Law that one must lose all to find all. Even as Buddha, one must eat of the lowly broth, walk the rocky byroads, feel the naked sun of humanity's sorrows before the Gold of the Elixir is showered upon one. So it was with me, when I left the Isle of Samos, after my initiation and awakening, when my psychic centers bore the light of Isis. I started on the blessed grueling Path of Mastership—to walk incognito among men, making myself known only to my trusted disciples.

"Yes, that is often the cross of the Master, and the glory —to be in the world, but not of it, to bear their mission, to give, to love, often unknown, unsung. Yet ever there are the few, the Cosmic Mate, the Beloved Friend and the Trusted Disciple, who create the joyous note, that compensation which ever comforts the Master's heart. If this were not so, Mastership could never be. Ah, yes, God Himself needs the love of man, and man the love of God— (one is all, all is one)—Master and pupil, aye, Master and life are interblended at every step of the Way. Plant, beast, human and divine—all are a part of the Master

Path."

Now the Green Hills, where the Master speaks, are hushed in cosmic silence. The Master smiles, and grave his tone, yet gentle with the beat of life.

"Pensatia, when again you meet me here, I will relate the second chapter of 'The Master H.' Fear not, obey; health is yours, and supply. Now it seems all is not, yet know all is. That which seems so dark has passed. Keep vigil here in cosmic green."

I heard his blessed words. They comforted and healed all pain. I knew by God's grace I would meet the Master and write his words.

chapter ☆ **TWO**

'Twas morning like spring in mountain dew. The song of birds rose with me to cosmic heights. I came upon the meadowed green of Akasha. There again came Blessed Master H.

"Heaven's greetings, Pensatia. Seat yourself here beside me on the grassy slope of fourth dimensional matter and write as I relate this second chapter.

"*Grace*, my student of the Rose, saw me through the many roads; aye, today Grace bestows upon me the seamless Robe. Great the crisis of this dying age into the Aquarian Cycle. All the Masters visible and invisible give their all to aid the human race.

"Back in other ages, aye, Atlantis, I, a son of the solitude, played well my part to keep the Flame of Isis alive and powerful for good. There I plied white magic pure and most holy good, plied I the sacred Word to bring forth, to heal, to bless—and when Atlantis sank beneath the waves, I Master H, by God's grace and my mission, which runs in my today, with *four and twenty* others, were safely journeyed to other lands—East, West, North and South. We were chosen to do our work, and obey we did. Yes, Pensatia, I labored in the Land of the Incas, in mighty Egypt, in Babylon's splendor, and on the sands of the Galilee. Always I followed my instructions from my Guru, he, tall and dark of eye and beard. Never did he command —never chided—only his eyes spoke when I was wrong, only the love in his voice, his words of understanding. 'Always,' he said, 'no matter the fall, the mistakes—it is the rising up which counts, the about-face. Arise, H, know each turnabout of man is a new birth. It is only when man becomes crystallized in stony negativeness in thought and action that one retrogrades and seems to stand still, perhaps for several lives.'

"Yes, Pensatia, I too did create a gap, a cycle of incarnations when I vegetated and wallowed in aimless living, even though within, my subconscious knew better, for my Master foundation was ingrained deep within; only my outer ego rebelled and would not heed. Yet cosmic destiny prevailed—and on the Wheel of Birth I broke my hardened shell and bore upward and on to my Master Role. And on the 'Bridge of San Luis Rey' came and passed those I had known and loved; they I was fated, by cause and effect, to know. The Panorama of Maya's duality ever sought to down me. Yet it is the Law—when the moment is ripe, all past karma is liquidated and one stands fresh and free to do their Master work.

"Pensatia, there is no joy or peace to compare in dedication to one's cosmic mission. This is the creative Word, the goal, for all humanity when they are ready. Disciples do not attain full Mastership even after their Guru leads them to the Holy Grail and then leaves them on their own. Now the disciple, the adept, must prove he can carry out his assignments cosmically given. Let me tell you—it is

not easy—for often one must give up home, country, love
and fortune, to obey. Such was one of my missions—to
walk incognito among the lowest of the Round, seemingly
—the derelicts, prostitutes, the criminally inclined, the
poor, the ignorant, unlettered. For one whole incarnation
I lived thusly, wearing my mantle of Samos, as an invisible power of Light, Life and Love—completely cut off
from friends, home and native country, and the high
courts of culture and learning. I became one with them,
yet apart.

"Yes, Pensatia, in the seething pot of life's underworld,
I played my part as cosmic mediator and brother to humanity's underdog. My Cordelia of Rose was my only
shield—the Eye of Shiva, my light to see into their hearts.
In that incarnation I met one youth, tall and clear-eyed,
of Inca blood. He became my disciple; and a woman of
the people also, she of Gypsy incarnation, a true Romany.
These two, out of the whole seething underworld, became
my trusted disciples. They loved, and I wed them by sign
of Rose and Cross. Even so it is fated they meet again and
wed in this life of today, or some other life, unless by
Grace otherwise. That it was my mission to draw them on
the Path of Mastership, I knew, and to plant the seed of
their today's meeting. For when with my blessing they set
voyage to the Land of the Incas, I too departed from this
incarnation, and in the Hall of the White Brethren, I made
my port of call—until, by free will I obeyed another call:
to aid man to step upon the Path to the Holy Mountain
of the Illuminati.

"Now in all lands are my few trusted disciples, they
who know my voice, they who will attain Mastership.
Those two, whom I had wed in my last incarnation I have
met again; they have met and inwardly their love is remembered. So it must be, they will wed again, unless freed
from karma—and even as their yesterdays, it will be beautiful and of soul passion. I watch, Pensatia, and aid daily,

the flowering of their love. He of the Incas will cultivate the Seed of the Rose sprouted so long ago by me and the Gypsy maid, in this or his next incarnation. So does cause and effect work—so do the Lords of Karma bring a meeting. Their hearts dare not refuse their meeting, for Gypsy blood and Inca's heart, those disciples of yesterday shall know and love today.

"I tell you this, Pensatia, to show that in a Master's life, to bring one person onto the Path is often the lone assignment of a Master. Yes, all that grueling mission incognito, was solely for the purpose of discipleship of these two lovers, destined again and yet again to wed—for such is the pull of a great and noble love.

"And there are many such matings on the rounds of incarnation—many, until on the Holy Mountain one meets the ultimate, the mating in the Alchemical Rose. This is a mystery only solved by initiation."

Now Master H stood tall and commanding on the green hill of infinite dimensions. He bore down upon me with his eyes of fiery wisdom, and in his hand I beheld the Rosy Cross most bright and golden and rosy red.

"Pensatia," and now his voice was soft and tender, "this is my talisman, my guide through my path of Holy Orders, given me by my Guru of Samos and by the Christus White. So let it be the symbol most loved by all disciples on the Master Path. Even as you lift your consciousness here to meet me, carry always in your heart the Lotus Bud and Rosy Cross, and Star of the Magi. Many will be the Beasts of the World, the Black Masters which seek to tear these credentials from you. Be vigilant and speak with fire of the Sword of Justice, when needed. Hold to the spirit of the Rose, and fear not, all will be well. Be faithful and write this Diary of my life. In it will be exposed truths of the Black Art, the inverted Path of White. Yet know, you will finish this and it will be published, even though it is not the desire of those who wear the cape of black. Fear not,

Pensatia; obey and write. Your supply, and all your needs, will come, and that which you desire will bless you. Heed it and regeneration must and will be a fact."

I heeded the Master's words, for all seemed indeed a dead end—only faith in God and my Master had kept me going. By God's grace I shall obey my assignment, come what may.

Now a soft wind hovered warm upon my heart, like a muted violin note. I felt the blessed pulse of the Rose, dawn and bless my writing of the Book of the Master. Now the silver waters of life rushed in mighty power before me . . . Master H as of yore spoke the Word, "Be still," and like a mirrored calm, all was still. "Kneel, Pensatia, and drink," he bade me. With him I did bare my lips to drink of the Sacred Stream, now so peaceful and still. As I did, the whole wide world was with me, and all I knew was Love.

The Master smiled. Again we sat upon the cosmic green . . .

"Pensatia, my next incarnation and assignment was high in the courts of the intelligentsia, the elite of France. There I planted seeds that shall play a potent part in the Aquarian Cycle we are entering. So work the Masters from Age to Age—giving, serving, igniting man to do and dare, to find and liberate the Holy Elixir and Stone. There in France before and during the Revolution I brought forth 12 secret disciples of the Path. They now are scattered in England, Egypt, America, China and India, and aye, in Alaska's snow lives one beyond them all. Pensatia, may you and others meet him—so I speak the word. Yes, there in this ordained state lives and works a Master of Cosmic renown. He now is working for peace, for the Shamballa of the Christus to come forth upon the earth. He is above me as the sun is above the earth. So this great one,—yes, Pensatia, he is my Guru of Samos, my blessed Master again on earth. We walk apart in our assignments, yet

together, ever Master and Disciple, one to the other—I
to pen through you, Pensatia, to inspire the brush of artist,
to stir the music of the spheres down to man, aye, also to
bring quick healing of heart and mind to those who ask.
My heart is wide, my love big. I guide because I have
climbed the dangerous passes, and won the purple mountains of Shangri-La. I have drank the bitter Waters, been
crucified, and passed through the Fire of Isis. Now with
true compassion I seek to aid and make less rough the
Disciple's Path.

"So mark well, Pensatia. Every Mastership won makes
easier the way for those who follow. Hence, always reverence those daring cosmic and earthly pioneers, for without
them evolution would be long indeed and most brutal-
ized."

Yes, many pages of cosmic roles fill the Master's many
lives. So closes this second chapter of "The Master H."

chapter ☆☆ **THREE**

The Master came. A yellow haze lay low upon the
green of our meeting place. I felt heavy in heart and soul;
I came hoping the Master would lift me up. He did—just
to see him, strong, wisdom-wise, walking toward me with
the Staff of Mastership.

"Pensatia," he spoke, "drink this." He offered me a
green and golden liquid in vial of crystal clear. A sip and
my earth cares seemed no more. I was ready to hear, to
heed and write.

"A Master in the making, even when a student or disciple—often low ebbs cover one; there are moments, aye,
days when Maya's dregs and Karma's heavy darts or the

earthly lacks surge upon one's mission and make one doubt, even that the Masters are. Aye, Pensatia, it comes to all, to me many times—the outside tempo, the masses proclaiming the way of all flesh. The difference between the Disciple and the Pretender is: the true student, the disciple, obeys through all odds and temptations—even through the mockery and indifference of those about him. For often incognito the disciple must walk the Master Path, doing his work unsung, unknown. But mark well my words, Pensatia, even as you and all obey assignments given, even so will the harvest come; even so thy deepest desire be granted. You will have gold to give, to serve, and white healing even when death seems near.

"Ah, yes, Pensatia, never doubt; the Guru, by God's grace ever watches and cares for the Beloved True Disciple. Often, life after life, through the miracle of regeneration, through the Master's touch I was lifted up to sip the Golden Dawn. My centers were unified with cosmic health flowing through my body temple; even so will it be for all who obey.

"Strange experiences; that is, strange to the ignorant, but of much wisdom to the student. Paradox of action by the Guru often made me wonder; often he stood afar coldly aloof, seeming not. Once I was stranded in the vast city of London, although I had my cosmic credentials and cash within my belt. I was robbed, beaten and left to die, like some alley cat; and all the Path seemed not; my Guru a myth, my assignment which I had come to London specifically to find was at a dead end. It was then, when breath seemed all but leaving my body, my beloved Guru came gently through the dark foggy night of London slums. He came and lighted the darkness; came and said 'Well done, disciple of my heart. This was your assignment. Behold the reason for what happened.' Through the mist of fog, a picture formed; saw I a beating and robbing of one in ages past; yes, a brutality was shown me, I as instigator. 'Even so,' spoke my Guru, 'is such meted out to you; thus it was powerless to avert. Such karma must be met before one walks ahead. Remember, brutality creates the same. It is finished now; love will generate the next meeting, for you will meet soon. And he who robbed and beat you will know you in another life as Master H, his Guru.'

"And so it is today. He is my right hand, my most youthful disciple, one who shall ever see that all I pen through you, Pensatia, is given to the world; even as he obeys, so shall all be. So you see, Pensatia, deeds come up in life only to wipe out old debts, or to renew old loves, or to quicken us to gain conscious immortality."

Now the Master turned, and a smile made bright his features. "Pensatia, know I am overshadowing that which is to be; soon the outflow, the action will be. Doubt not, have faith, the way is opened now. Before autumn passes, it will be."

My heart leaped with joy. I knew the Master's words were true.

"Yes, Pensatia, and every neophyte or student of the Way—even so did my Guru of Samos tell me things along the Way, and ever did they come to pass. Yes, there are moments when the Master's word or promise makes deep desires come to pass. For remember, it is God's will to create happiness, love and peace along the Master Path. If such is written on the Cosmic Chart, even so do the Masters at appointed moments bring quick answers. So rejoice even when all seems not, when the opposite seems true—it is then one may know the hour is at hand when that desired will come forth. Even as it was with me, and all the Masters to be, even so it is with all who walk the Path; their deep desire will be gratified.

"To go back to my History . . . Even when I had attained the Master's Cape, even when I made gold and gave gold, I was assigned to most humble roles. In dirt and squalor again I pitched my tent in darkest Africa. I, Master H, incognito walked among the fields where now are great diamond mines . . . In Lama guise in Tibet I scanned its karmic chart and did much to leaven its ancient cross . . . I lived in India, a master astrologer, a Yogi of cosmic credentials. Today disciples there still heed me as their Guru . . . I tell you, Pensatia, that the world might know, a Master's Path is many rounds, many ups and downs; that only to a trusted few does a Master ever reveal himself, and then only to aid, quicken the evolution of man, and to bring to pass the desires when earned. I was known under many names and dress, from royalty to plebeian commoner, from beggar to country squire. Patriots bore my name, and I—a noted pioneer—aided the trail to the West.

"Yes, Pensatia, so do I appear, and live through many ages bearing my Master signature. I today bear witness to the cusp of this Aquarian age. My square cut beard of gray has weathered many climes. As I appear to you, Pensatia, so do I appear to all my disciples reincarnated now. Yet when advisable I can and do assume my various incarnations—such as now . . ."

I looked. Where Master H stood, now was a tall dark turbaned stranger with yogic robe of India. Only his eyes bore recognition to my soul. As quickly he changed to high cast Chinese Buddhist Master; only a smile made my heart know it was my beloved Master H. Now a gnarled and aged man with ragged cape stood before me asking alms—then a lean stripling with deep eyes of Master vision. I knew it was Master H in his first incarnation at the Isle of Samos. An Italian nobleman came forth, a Pope of history, a statesman of Greece, a noble Aztec chief. I pondered there on Heaven green—even as my Guru assumed his today's character.

He spoke: "I now am the sum total of them all. I manipulate my attributes of yesterday in my todays. Yet,

as you sensed—all is really one. Such is the awakening of
memory and sojourn in the Hall of Records, such is the
Law—the tools of yesterday become the power of our
todays. So, neophytes, disciples, bear well within thy yesterdays, study, gaze into the Hall of Records and see
without fear thy cause and effect. For such is the Law of
the Path."

Now a glow of memory accentuated his features, a deep
pain etched his eyes. "Note and heed, Pensatia, my
amanuensis: in seeking Mastership, even when almost one
attains, many a bout with the masters of the Black Art
crosses thy path. Many a guise of alluring temptation
comes one's way. For subtle Satanic black magic ever
tries to woo one from the Path. So it was with me. I was
sent on a high White assignment where wealth and beauty
prevailed. A woman of dazzling charm and form had a
wide following in a village in the mountains of France.
Back in ages now since dim, my work was to meet and destroy her Satanic rites. For all the villagers were hypno-
tized under her inverted power; ignorance came and sat
at her door and obeyed her commands. Their wealth, labor
of their hands, their lands, all came to her—then death
mysteriously crept upon them. This could not last. I Master H, young in Mastership, but with ardent heart, set out
to still the Devil's brew. I tell of this black mark upon my
history to warn you, Pensatia, and all disciples, to be ever
on your guard, that such be not your lot. O pain, sorrow
and new karma to liquidate fell upon me in that incarnation. Yes, until Mastership wears the infallible signature
of the triune Jewel of Isis and the six-pointed Hexagram
ingrained in equality from heart to head, there is ever pos-
sibility of succumbing to the Black Art. And how one pays
for such digression! For it is written in Akasha, when in
knowledge one slips off and drinks of the under waters,
for that incarnation one can be cut-off from attaining all
desires earthly and heavenly—only memory gnaws at

one's vitals that a heavy sorrow holds one down. Only penance, sacrifice and turning solely to God can bring peace. Yet if students bear with love and patience, their close of life will be remarkable and wondrous. Such is the grace and mercy of the Creator.

"To resume . . . Her name, does it matter? I, a Master new with my credentials, was putty—like any country stripling. I became a devotee, I swore by Rose and Cross my cosmic orders were wrong; she was no devil's child but a white saint, a crucified giver of good. I met her 'brother' —yes, even now I shudder to recall how hoodwinked I was. He was her lover and daemonic master in the Black Mass. Together they cast their unholy illusions about me —sought to crown me one of their own. Murder, lust, every conceivable perversion of white magic did I learn and follow in that blot in my history. Yet at the close, my Guru came, saying, 'H, even though you have failed your assignment and wallowed in orgies of satanic negation, because of your record before, I say you have learned your lesson, which all must learn—never to be side-tracked from your cosmic orders. Remember, all help is given the disciple as long as he obeys, and even when he falls; yet by his own strength he must cling to the esoteric path of the White Brethren.' I, H, sought to throw away all my credentials, aye, my Cross and Rose; like a gangling fool, I fell for earth power, fleshly lust, and to enslave my fellow man. It all seemed at first so angelic. She, as woman can, created the illusion that this was the Master Path, aye, the Black Mass to me was all, such is the power of woman, inverted.

"Yes, my Guru came as I was dying, ragged, alone, an outcast, a murderer. It was they or me. I will say with my eyes opened at the last, I realized my stain upon the Rose, and did rise and with a cry to the God of my heart and my Master of Samos. I was given the Sword of Justice and destroyed the unholy Black Mass in that village of France.

And because of that last gesture, and my penance as I was dying in self-made cause, my beloved Guru came and did lay the Rose and Cross in my hand, and chanting the esoteric OM, he, by grace of my high record, did there and then liberate my karmic blot, and as I made my transition, he spoke: 'H, you will come back stronger and ever after invulnerable to the Black Arts. Never again will this experience be repeated; you have suffered and paid the price through sorrow and true penance. You are forgiven even as those who were instruments in your downfall. Remember, God is just; He ever adds the sum total and then by grace and mercy one's self-made prison is lifted and one is free to carry on and up the Master Road.'

"So, Pensatia, with peace upon my heart, the baptismal waters poured over me and I crossed the River Styx, the fragrant Rose upon my breast. Thus it is I ever shadow my disciples. For mark well, Pensatia, very few disciples fall as I did. True, by God's grace and my Guru's love, I liquidated my weakness, and strength ever more was ingrained in me. Now with special compassion, I aid those drawn close to the brink of the Black Masters; those who ply occult power for self and gain, and perversion Satanic. Yes, that is part of my mission—to make strong my disciples. A true student on the Master Path must have the integration, the heart wisdom, the one-pointedness to stand foursquare and know the black from the white and vice versa. It was only by grace of my past record and obedience that a cosmic accounting liberated this blot upon my climb to cosmic consciousness. Yet by that drastic suffering and exposure I became a Master truly made in the crucible of Hell. Out of that initiation the dross was eliminated. A Master rose with understanding and wearing the Cape of Power earned. I humbly state, from then on my incarnations to the present in my today bear witness to my obedience to my Lord and to my beloved Guru of Samos. Never does my Friend, now living in Alaska, speak of that dark episode; only his eyes tell me how valiantly I have won my Master's robe. Never again will I have to relate so sad an incarnation; yet in writing this, my failings must be penned even as my triumphs. It is my prayer, Pensatia, that all my disciples be strong and hold to Rose and Cross when the dark Master steps across their path.

"How will you know him—Pensatia, you ask? That is for another chapter. Return now to earth vibration. I will speak of that when we meet again."

And there, tall, broad of shoulder, went Master H across the Heaven green. Never have I seen such nobility and strength of cosmic grace. God aid us all to be as honest.

chapter ☆ **FOUR**

The sky was black and stormy. Angry red heat blistered everywhere. Again I raised my consciousness to green cosmic land. There my beloved Guru, Master H, greeted me as of yore.

"Pensatia, lay all aside and heed and pen my words," said he. "Now, to resume with our History, I believe you asked: How does one recognize the Black Masters, or they who ply the dark arts? I will tell you, that ever you, Pensatia, and others may be on guard.

"Their appearance is most beautiful, most commanding to behold. Often they look to be saintlike and oh, so good. They present all that is cosmic and holy, and by their subtle music and outward glamour they woo the neophyte, aye, the young Master, to feel the stern disciplines of the Path, the initiations, the crucible, the Alchemist's Bench, is not needed. They ever whisper: There is a shorter way

—that orgy of the senses, the power of material gold is essential. Yes, they, as spider's web, are cunning in their perverted use of the White Light, the nether side; aye, it was the cause of Atlantis' fall, beneath the waves of yesterday. Not until the students of Master timber are well up the ladder do the Black Masters seek to pull them down. Yes, until one wears the seamless Robe of the fabled Stone and Elixir, there are ever the wanton ones, the sires of negation. Only the Lighted Candle in thy heart and a holding to the Rose and Cross will avail against the Devil's Mass. Ah, Pensatia, if in that great temptation I had held to the Rose—if I had ever heeded the Christus in my heart, I would not have had to pay that bitter karma, so long ago.

"So at every step of the Way, disciple, be not lured by appearances of Maya's glamour; be not swayed by brilliant intellect and outward beauty, which has no heart. Remember, wisdom and goodness and Mastership often cloak ugly exteriors which become truly beautiful when recognized. By this infallible law, learned only through pain and tears, is the real disciple and Master known—by obedience, childlike faith in God, a warm love to all that lives and blessings to those who seek to destroy. Yes, ever Christ the Blackness, but enter not into it. For know the black art is helpless in the light of Love divine. I forgot to hold my Christ light, forgot all save the most beautiful exteriors of she who craved only passion of the flesh and not of soul, craved only to have outer gold, the tinsel of Maya's illusions.

"Think not, Pensatia, always the intelligentsia, the wealthy, the aristocracy of blood hold the servant of our Lord. Often in so-called Skid Row, my most trusted disciples are found, they who like Magdalenes arise and follow all the way. Often they who hold no college diplomas dare to climb the cosmic way and win the Star, the Rose, the Lotus Crown of the Illuminati. They learn from God's

own heart, aye, they read from the Book of Life, in Nature's heart, by love only they learn its sacred secrets. O
students, disciples, bear thy Christ light, and be you man
or woman, you can walk the underworld of crime and
remain untouched; one can sup with prostitutes, aliens
from afar. Yes, even a Master of the Black cannot touch
you, as long as you protect yourself in Circle of Gold and
ever wear your Robe of White or keep upon your heart
the Rosy Cross. Integration in the center alone is the talisman against all delay and negation of the Path. O rugged
is the Master Path, I Master H know too well—a path of
fire, earth, air and water to master and become the victor,
a path of sorrow and the cross, yet a path of immortality
of consciousness. Upon it Solomon walked; the Magda-
lene, disciple of the Avatar Jesus, the Christed one;
Boehme, the gentle shoemaker; Swedenborg; Tom Paine;
Pythagoras, that Grand Master of yesterdays lives today
I know; so do my disciples, Bacon, Alden of the Rose, way
showers of the Path—they lighted the Way of Rose and
Cross. Before the Holy Ghost pours over, through and in
one's blood and bone, one must climb the winding path
around the mountain of the Gods, there where the sacred
fire of initiation awaits he who climbs into that high white
mist where the Elixir and Stone is born.

"It was in that last incarnation to this today, I made the
top, the last leap up and through the dangerous pass. I
drew my cordelia tight and sounded the Holy OM, and
with my Rosy Cross I crossed in safety the Bridge of
Vision and walked into infinite peace. I stood profoundly
still, in the wondrous Golden Flame; I beheld the Sacred
Stone guarded by angels three, and lo, she, my beloved
came, and together we conceived and bore the Stone to
Life.

"Yes, Pensatia, pen these words—I Master H walked
the tightrope to Mastership, and even as I, so you and all
can and will on life's many rounds do likewise. There on

that highest mountain pass, there where a thousand volt-
age of cosmic waters roar, I braved alone only with my
Rosy Light, the ring of all the planets, and did make the
grade into my esoteric chart. Now no astrological mundane rays influence me; I am guided only by the Holy
Grail and my esoteric light. Still the Guru of Samos, he
my Friend, Brother of the Third Degree, who in Alaska's
cold serves to bring forth the seed of a new tomorrow,
meets me at will. In my body of Light I come and go, come
to my disciples; in inner awareness they know and sense
me. Though I still use my physical body, I can discard or
dwell in it as needed; I master it, not it me. Regenerated,
I enjoy all things of Heaven and earth, for Maya enslaves
no more. I am alone, beyond all duality; all relationships,
beast, bird, plant, humans gravitate to my aura, which has
naught but love, compassion, mercy. I walk with my
gnarled staff of cosmic and earthly Mastership, incognito
save to a treasured few; I bring to pass true desire to those
who ask in faith. Ask now, O readers, and receive. Three
times three be thy requests—yes, you who ask, know before the day is over, thy prayer is answered.

"Heed, Pensatia, write—meet me here, and even as the
ravens fed Elijah, even so will the Cosmic care for all who,
even when all seems not, press on, obeying, even when all
earthly props seem swept away. It is then in Cathedral of
the Soul, may thou go and meet thy God, ask and give
thanks that even as the lilies of the field know the Father's
care and bounty, even so shall man."

O what wondrous comfort the Master's words! I spoke:
"Beloved Master H, God give me Light to pen this book
of you, the Master."

He smiled, "You will, Pensatia. Now let us speak no
more of the Black Brethren; they are to be loved, forgiven
and pitied, for alas, they only in the end destroy themselves. Ever seek to see the inner signature of all; when in
doubt, stand still in thy center and hold to the Rose and

Cross, and all lesser things will pass. Storms, loss and Maya's winds may blow—but it will not come nigh thy dwelling, nor thy people. The outer will pass, but the inner will bring forth pure gold.

"Now Pensatia, on my Path of Mastership, in one incarnation I lived and learned solely from Nature, and its spirits, the elves, sylphs, fairies, the voice of flower, tree and stream. I lived among the beasts of the wild, and in love—we spoke a common tongue. So now in my today, in love they serve me. Yes, Pensatia, on the round of discipleship and the Master road, nature must be wooed and won, that all of earth and heaven lie ingrained in living experience, in thy heart's consciousness. At the needed moment, herbs and Nature's talisman, and earth essence, is given the disciple, even as it was given me; in the night when slumber covered me, Nature came and made strong my physical body. Even so shall it do for you and all who take the Master Path. Often I was told to walk where all was chaos and turmoil. Yet remember, if willing to obey, it is then golden showers descend and give you all. No disciple of the Path, at a certain round, is put where his work or mission is interrupted, neither at the well-earned job is one left stranded without supply. Yes, once I had been given an assignment, and suddenly without notice my earth supply was taken away. Nothing there was but seemingly dependence on Him. Aye, obeying my mission in youth, I turned to the source, the God within, and my Master of Samos. 'Thy will be done, show me, Lord, what thou would have me do,' was my prayer, my plea. And lo, came back the answer, 'Obey, fear not, at the last moment Gold will come.' And so it did, and thus it will for all who walk the age-old Rosy Path.

"Remember, when one is given an assignment, at first the way is rugged, all things happen; all seem to whisper to let go, to take the easy way, even when one lays hold in earnest. To do and dare when every earthly supply—

love, money, health suddenly seems low and no more. Then, Pensatia, and all disciples, students—arise and face the East; cry out to the I Am, the OM, and say: 'All that the Father has is mine.' Give thanks and let not a day go past that you do not lay a brick on thy sacred assignment. Even so, rest and know thy debts, thy living will be assured. Aye, thou will have full measure running over, to give and share; out of the blue will come gold, earned in ages past or in the now."

The Master became silent. With folded arms he scanned the cosmic horizon, and pink dew mist fell over the green meadowed hill. Music, soft harmonic melody, swelled upon the air. The pause, the silence seemed most holy long. Then the Master turned, arose and drew his cape of gold about him, and his aura dazzled like the sun. He offered me an essence bright, of clear red—a drop he infused within my veins, by touch. Behold, I felt new life, strength—an alchemical change, with healing taking place.

"Pensatia, even so on Isle of Samos did my Guru infuse the life essence of the red. I needed it on earth to do my work; even so do you, as do all who walk the Master Path."

Also, he handed me a green leaf, spicy and of rare aroma—a subtle glow silhouetted it. "Take this, Pensatia, and treasure this cosmic herb. It aids regeneration of body, mind and soul illumined. On earth, Pensatia, sometimes its duplicate will be given you, and all my students, even as it was given me so long ago, many incarnations past. Wherever pain comes, place it and ask for healing; it will come. May all have faith, and obey; night will pass. The Golden Dawn will come. Share always with humanity, and when love beckons, leave all and follow, even though of worldly goods one has naught, for supply will come if love be true and God comes first. My beloved who, so long ago, tore my heart apart through parting, only to afterwards meet in cosmic garden—lives again in my today.

We are of equal Mastership, negative-receptive, intuition and wisdom mated eternally. Yes, we walk and work together, she to step in at sudden intervals, when my disciples need quick action, quick aid. Yes, Pensatia, you have thought rightly, it is she, the beautiful dark Italian Master, she my beloved and one of the woman Masters of all who walk the aged Path of Cosmic Consciousness. Ah, yes, Pensatia, without her I could not have made the grade. Noble Margaret, of the few women Masters, she obeyed and attained; now one by one, all will sense her when needed and in dire crisis. For mark well, Pensatia, never does man or woman gain Cosmic Consciousness without their complement in Mastership. Both are needed on the Wisdom Path. I write this through you, Pensatia, to tell you of all the blessed moments in my many lives. The meeting again on earth of my lovely Margaret is my blessing and cosmic strength. Even so, students, call, in your heart make your plea—she will hear. Ask what you will, it will be granted; yet ever say, 'Thy will be done'—ask not to hurt another."

Even as he spoke, I did obey, and in my heart's vision came she, the illustrious M, walking softly on the cosmic green, making the sign of aged Rose and Cross. She sat beside the Master H.

"Yes, Pensatia," smiled he the Guru, "this attainment of woman is possible for all, yet I admit few make it, for the Path is more rugged for woman than man. For that positive power of Ra must be awakened and mate with Ma, the unified Light, that Alchemical Marriage. Yet women must and shall earn the Master's role even as blessed Margaret, she of dark and lustrous hair and eyes."

Spoke beloved Margaret: "Upon this fourth dimensional green meadowed hill, I come to lay my love and blessing upon these pages of your past, and into your today and tomorrow, which is only one."

Turning to me, in tender cadence she spoke: "Pensatia,

in many lives I watered the Way for H, came at the forks of the Path, and with my intuitional love I gently took his hand (as I do all disciples, when ready) and pointed to the Star of the Holy Grail, and bade him follow then. He listened, heeded, as many never do in many rounds, and in walking on the Master Path, I granted by God's grace a desire inbred deep within his heart, and departed. Thereafter, he ever held the Staff of the Hidden One within his hand, and never stopped his climb to Pilgrim's Rest high in Shangri-La. Yes, there is a Holy sweet moment when I come to all disciples and ever offer a new power; strength is theirs, and even so is granted long unfulfilled desires."

She, the Master Woman, arose. "Pensatia, it will be; never doubt though all seems otherwise; know, I have spoken—for you, and all who read this book of the Master H, in sincerity and open heart."

A subtle aroma as of rose petals permeated throughout Heaven's meadow whereupon we sat. Margaret the glorious was gone. A profound hush prevailed; Master H seemed in deep contemplation, unaware of me and everything.

At last he spoke, in subdued, sonorous tone: "Well I remember that incarnation. It was a dark and stormy day in the Isle of the White Cliffs of Dover, back in the year —well, does it matter—it was when Knighthood was in flower, when Nature made lush the land. Aye, I wore my Master Cape; it was most new and cosmic shining. O blessed White Cliffs of Dover, O great green trees of England; to this day nostalgia pulls me into my yesterdays— those golden days when she came to me, when so young upon the Master Path and deed, there in merry England, came she, alive to me once more out of the cosmic garden, where we had talked so often and roamed the flowered paths in soul consciousness—now in Master consciousness and earth incarnation, came she to grace my Mastership. Yes, we were wed in that legendary land where Robin

Hood and the Knights of the Round Table held sway.

"Yes, Pensatia, Masters marry. Not until one goes into
the Cosmic Third Degree and beyond does one of own
free choice discard physical mating. Yet remember well,
Pensatia, it is use, not abuse, of all rounds of physical
experiences that creates the Master consciousness. There
in England's long ago, we bore two sons, who, even as I
in Chaldea, were disciplined early on the Wisdom Path.
Even though my cosmic work was incognito, that earth
reunion with my mate, our life and home, was, and is a
vast warm oasis of memory ever alive within my heart. A
plague ravaging the foggy Isle took our sons, and naught
of my cosmic learning could stay the gong of the Hidden
One. Yet, knowing that death is only an initiation into
life, we moved our consciousness often to cosmic garden,
and there flowered as one stream, in love and joy.

"Yes, Pensatia, never grieve for those who pass beyond
the prison body. We miss the physical touch, the earthly
companionship, but seek and know there is the rarer altitude of meeting and loving, so far above and beyond the
earth vibrational contact, there is no comparison. Now
today they are reincarnated, one in America, a humble
farmer of intelligence and inner wisdom brought over
from his master tutelage. He lives close to mother earth,
woos her streams and woods, and all who know him, speak
of him as friend to man and beast. I know he was my noble
son, though we have not met as yet. When the time is ripe,
he will know. Yet ever I overshadow and watch. The other
son, our youngest, lives in far-off Italy, trained in Papal
circles, a mystic clear and true, strong and clean of limb.
He is to be in later years canonized a Saint. I stand afar
and watch, wait and pray they attain the mountain top,
and the chalice of Rose and Cross.

"Now at the close of that epochal life in England, the
hour arrived when we, Margaret and I, were ordered to
the mountain air of the Lords of Karma. There in the rare-

fied mist of the Rose, we made our choice to hence discard physical union, and rise into the noble Third Degree. In infinite embrace, rising in our bodies of Light, we took the solemn pledge: to work for mankind, to serve our Guru and the Holy Grail, to be parted and yet together, yet know no land our home, no hearth fire permanent. In the spiral of the gold, in the raiment of the purple of High Mastership we severed allegiance to all earthly ties, and each bore our way to our earthly missions, now unfettered, free, yet together in Alchemical Fire. We have no regret for taking the esoteric, noble Third Degree. Today, Pensatia, I Master H take the color wherever I walk, wear the garb most suited to the occasion. Only a few recognize my Mastership, and they by eye alone, for always in the eye is seen the inner signature of man and Master. There and there only, rising from the flame of the heart, glows the sacred mark of the Master, there power when earned is born and heals, blesses, loves by the gaze of Isis."

chapter ☆ FIVE

The Master was waiting in cosmic green. The air was most holy, most clear and of softly rosy hue . . .

"Write, Pensatia—heed and use, for truth infallible from records of Akasha, I now relate. It is apropos to speak of love and infatuation, and how to know reality. I speak of this, for know, Pensatia, on the Master Path all must recognize Love. Remember, there is an ultimate affinity for all humanity; yet in attaining that grand passion triune, know, it often takes many lesser loves to make the whole. Every one is a milestone on the Wisdom Path. Every true love—not infatuation—is the tuning relationship of soul consciousness, and prepares one for the ultimate mating on the mountain top of illumination. Through the many rounds of the Path, we meet those drawn to us from past ties; many are like ships that pass in the night; karma involved is finished in meeting—a faint nostalgia only stirs the heart. Yet others create fateful mating. When this happens, biological difference in age matters not; neither race, creed nor barriers of any kind can keep the inevitable marriage from coming to pass. The inner recognizes and obeys. Love is different from infatuation; it is silent, hard to express—only eyes reveal; often indifference marks the true. Know, if a woman loves, the eyes speak out, and if returned, the eyes answer—with steady gaze and a uniting, then and there is pledged that which must be fulfilled objectively. Poverty, age, all obstacles are broken when the Lords of Karma sound out: This will be.

"Yes, on the Master Path Love met me, and I wed, and it was good and blest. Remember, lack of education, or wealth, cannot keep true love apart, even though the reverse often appears so. Heed not the outer, be frank, let the heart's fire go to the loved one, the Golden Flame, and though all seems contrary, that love must and will flower.

"A man, when deeply in love, finds expression difficult; the woman by faith must encourage the outer expression. For real love is ever humble and most reverent. Infatuation usually is bold and impressed by the physical only; it never lasts, and if it does, it is sex slavery only. Yet on the rounds of life's incarnations many times we are caught in infatuation's net, and learn the hard way. Such marriages are karmic, and our teachers. Real love is sired from soul and heart and mind—sex finds its expression lastly and is blest by the Light of Isis. Love is not dependent on equality of age, money, beauty, or anything outward. It is a meeting, a surging forth of soul and heart impelled to unite. It is so powerful, one stands humbly awed. Only with the knowing of the eyes, the inner surrender of the heart, does the man speak out. Always remember when a man truly loves, often he is outwardly gruff, indifferent; the woman, unless in her heart she knows, often feels unloved. Yet let her look long into his eyes and love will speak therefrom. That is cosmic law—Love is known from eye to eye before the outer speaks. One may live a life-time, and the years go by; suddenly he or she comes across the 'Bridge of San Luis Rey'—eyes meet, and souls, and the gong sounds, and all the stars and the Word proclaim 'This will be.' When love beckons, leave all and follow, yet be sure; read from the eyes and if the gaze is deep and steady and each locks with the other and one feels lifted up, know it is good. Know also, such love will find a way, even though often camouflaged by roughness and indiffer-ence. Yes, love is masked, often wounds until it comes out in the open. Know, time will reveal the gentle heart. Let woman ever flow the Golden Flame to the Heart of the Beloved, and neither Heaven nor Hell can prevent the wed-ding."

Now the Master turned, speaking low, yet vibrant, clear . . .

"Remember, banked love must burst forth, speak and unite—such is cosmic law across time, space; through in-finite waters comes love. One knows because a great still-ness prevails. Only the eyes meet and truth everlasting is proclaimed. Though the outer for a time may deny, yet not for long, else illness comes, for to deny one's mate creates negative karma, often through many incarnations. Thus, when love beckons, follow; yet infatuation give not in to. Friendship is often the hidden bud of love which suddenly blossoms."

Now Master H arose and all the hills of Heaven be-came most luminous. He turned, speaking . . .

"Remember, all karmic threads must be woven into the whole. Every relationship which impinges on one's aura must be met with love and understanding. Even so one must let go in consciousness, able to embrace all things and yet not possess. That is the one essential of Mastership—non-possession and faith absolute, in the source, to bring forth all needs and to heal. This comes step by step as one obeys, and climbs steadily within, to one's Holy Center.

"Pensatia, my tutelage was like a patch quilt of many colors; now brilliant, somber, or of gentle soft shades, all at last fitting into the seamless robe of Gold. In one life, even though my intellect knew, my heart still slept. It took many lessons to learn supply is not material but spiritual; unless the inner flow becomes our awareness, there will ever be lack, no matter how earthly rich one is.

"I remember back in the Hills of Judea, when Hebrew, studying the Torah and esoteric Kabbala. Money was plentiful, also land and outer prestige. Even though my intellect conversed with all the esoteric wisdom, I was enslaved by the material. I met Jesus, the Christed One, and did leave the orthodox, the Hebrew demagogues, became a disciple of the Christ, traveled to India, Tibet and mighty Egypt in his tutelage. I learned at his feet, as we all must learn, the awakening of the Heart Center, and the Gethsemane of the Cross, and in that life the glorious resurrection came forth for me a reality. I knew there is only life everlasting, abundant and fulfilling. In Egypt, I lingered. Jesus, the Christed One, came back to fulfill his cosmic destiny. From Egypt I sailed again to Isle of Samos. My Guru met me in the Sacred Grove of that fabled Isle. There I had a rare interlude, an oasis of rest and companionship with my blessed Guru. There my trusted disciple who is now trusted guardian of your pen was brought by I Master H, and true were his steps upon the Path. Then at Samos, Pensatia, through the esoteric Jade Mirror was revealed the print of his today's mission, ignited as a seed upon his soul memory—yes, your name, your works, his part—all were etched in Akasha, into this today. Thus it was, your meeting, your partnership and his vow to see that all my writings through you are published. He has been Chinese, Arabian, aye, Mongolian; he marched with Attila the Hun, was an American statesman, an Indian of royal rank, a Gypsy chief, a humble farmer on the Italian hills. Yes, many characters wove through his incarnations. He knew and learned from the Rosicrucian Cagliostro, Nostradamus, and the imperial St.-Germain. Now still, he is my most trusted disciple, and if in this incarnation he obeys, will yet wear the Master's Crown. Trust him fully —never will he betray you or the Rose. Fulfillment on all points of the Triangle will yet be his.

"I speak of this to reveal nothing happens by chance, all weaves into a cosmic purpose. Every friction, opposition, obstacle is a stepping stone to one's cosmic destiny. One incarnation when young upon the Path, under strict discipline, silence was the hardest attribute to acquire. Yet it is inevitable before Mastership. Silence is the door to Cosmic Consciousness. Silence in oppression, when ridiculed, and false gossip ensues—silence when crucified, silence at the dead end streets. If this is learned and ingrained in the crucible of training, then know for a surety Mastership will be one's crown.

"So, Pensatia, and you who aspire to the Wisdom Path, be silent; ask, know it will be. Know also, in reality there is no illness. All is harmony, health, love and fulfillment. Enslavement to Maya and earth vibrations creates the illusion of such—which seems real, and can if persisted in destroy one's body. When such comes upon one, rise in the Golden Flame and declare thy wholeness. It must come forth. When staying in the Gold, outer medication is not needed, for all nature and heaven are in the Golden Flame. Ask what you will in the Gold—it must come forth. In this esoteric Flame all is equalized. It regenerates, brings the elixir of youth and the power to function in all earthly relations. It steadies, purifies, brings beauty, and regeneration to all organs, glands; sleep, work, love in it for it is the wine of the Rose. In the Golden Flame everything is. Live unafraid in its cosmic vibrations. All is objectified in the Gold, and through the Gold, for the Flame flows eternally from the Creator's heart and down through man and nature. Yet unless awakened in the Heart, one cannot work consciously therein. Before Mastership comes one must be able to stand within this Flame and declare the Word. One may take minerals, vitamins—yet it is not necessary—for the green essence of earth is contained within it. Remember, Pensatia, the Golden Flame fulfills; the longer the stay in it, the more stabilized and rejuvenated one becomes.

"Start on the Master Path, reader; brave the crucibles and await thy summons from your Guru and the God of your Heart to walk, love and work in this immortal Flame. There will come that Holy moment, never doubt. Just build thy foundation, strong and pure be thy motives. When arriving there, know, the Elixir comes forth vivifying every part of thy earthly temple. Heart, lungs, all organs become whole slowly and surely; all signs of age disappear. For the esoteric essence of earth and Heaven circulates through blood, bone and all—this quintessence levels and calms and brings inner poise and wisdom. The flow of the Holy Ghost is it—every mundane activity falls into its natural value; long bodily complaints, weakness, pass; glands become young; hair, eyes, circulation benefits; all surplus fat goes; muscles become firm, body becomes toned up.

"The Golden Flame is fulfillment of the Master Path. Yet remember, never enter until one has passed through fire, air, earth and water, and entered the Heart Center. Only then is it safe to live in it. This is the potent secret of the ages; through it one attains the fabled Stone and Elixir.

"Now, in closing this chapter, this mandate goes forth: Seek the Path, do and dare, and there will come a time when even as I you will be bidden to walk and live in the Golden Flame. Henceforth, all you need will come, when the Gong sounds. So ask well. At times if one feels nausea, weakness, know it will pass; it is the purging of the Gold; only stay in it. Live naturally, knowing herein one is able to serve and objectify one's cosmic mission; one's soul power comes forth. Remember, when naught seems to come from thy asking in the Flame—days, aye, months, may pass—yet keep faith and vigil in the Gold. When least expected, all comes to pass."

The Master journeyed on, even as he came. His words echoed across the cosmic green, "Until the next chapter, Pensatia, peace be yours and all."

chapter ☆☆ S I X

Now the Master came, serene and tall with noble mien. We stood together beside a cosmic stream. The air was soft with Rose dew.

Turning, the Master spoke: "On the Master Path I learned as all must, to obey, to serve in act and thought through heart and soul, and always one-pointed—the Goal was the shining Grail. Even when my Guru gave me tasks seemingly unpleasant, ugly to the eye; even when karma bore me down to Hell, I put my hand to the plow, and weeds self-grown I cut from my path, and did plant the seeds of cosmic consciousness. For one whole incarnation I lived with earth and nature, learned to speak with the elements and beasts of the wild, learned the signature of herbs, the affinity of jewels, and the esoteric white magic of talismans. All this, Pensatia, must be learned in some life upon the Wisdom Road.

"In this incarnation I learned to depend only on nature and the Lord, learned to speak with primitive tongue, to stabilize all in the green essence of earth. There in virgin dark Africa, I by my Guru's request, studied and became initiated by a medicine man and chief of an alien race. I learned in every race, every age, esoteric wisdom is never forgotten. Being grounded in nature, and the tutelage of earth in the raw builds a foundation of strength needed at some point on the climb to illumination. Remember, equal balance of polarity of infinite and finite must be experienced in bone and fiber and blood of every disciple, before Mastership is attained. Slow and sure, only by obedience and laying brick by brick the edifice within, brings illumination.

"It was my task one whole incarnation to prepare for the next round. Left alone by my Guru in the silence and depth of nature in the wilderness, I learned to survive by love and instinct and adoration for wisdom, and the turning of nature's book. Thus it is, in my today, Pensatia, I read nature as well as the infinite, and both are one. I read the heart signature of all and see beneath Maya's illusion. I heal and bring forth when the student has earned such. Even so now, Pensatia, I would say aid comes and healing and new inspiration to him who was far on the Path so long ago. He will rise from the ashes of the past and stand foursquare in the sun. Even so will all come forth for her my trusted disciple, she who knows Samos even as I.

"As one becomes integrated in the Gold, one may sip at all tables, walk all streets, aye, in the underworld itself. For it is written in the Akashic Records: One who lives, works and loves in the Golden Flame transmutes and lifts up all he contacts. In love, the physical becomes sublimity and even a kiss given means regenerating healing, spiritual awakening to the one given. One's aura becomes powerful, expansive and far reaching. One month of steady living in the Flame of Gold brings noticeable regeneration of man or woman. They become one with the Gold. Glands, cells, organs, arteries, all become youthful and full of light. Even if one mates with one of lesser development. In the Gold, all are lifted up in some degree on the ladder of illumination. Incognito, through many relationships, the disciple works and serves God and the Masters, and while partaking of earth and the physical, he is master and not the slave of Maya. Here in the Golden Flame old loves are greeted; often they wed again, or else salute each other and pass like ships in the night. If fated to come together, no barriers matter, it will be. In the Gold, one may sip of all earth's gifts—in moderation. For that is the Law of Isis: use and not abuse of all life's physical functions. If at times a great weakness comes over one, know it is only the regenerating flow of the Gold through thy body; at such moments, stay on, it will pass and new life is assured. All must be able to stand and live in the Flame of Gold. It is impossible to grow old and live in the Flame of Gold. It is the secret of the ages. Yet remember, all who bathe in it have earned the right; they have passed the discipline of the Path, braved the crucibles; they have built the foundation. Slowly, surely they have heard the summons to henceforth live and work in the Gold. So will their work become potent and creative now. Their heart center awakened becomes unified with the flow of Gold as it pours through the head center and the eye of Shiva. So, neophytes, dare, do and be silent, and walk the Path of Rose. Keep thy vigil and when the time is ripe you too will walk in the Flame of Gold and be regenerated.

"So passed one round of my life in the tutelage of the Master Path. In that round I lived in the dense green of nature among primitive tribes. There I passed in transition and awaited in cosmic dimensions my call to resume my Master role on earth. This time I came back in India and was a Yogi on the foothills of the Himalayas. I read men's hearts, aided and taught my disciples near and far. All the many yogas I had mastered. Thus I gave as I was given in that life. I met again he who serves me now and the God of his heart; he who will publish to the last book all written through Pensatia. We met and again he was my most beloved disciple; yet he will know my face in this life, when he adds a new note in experience. Remember, I have spoken: in the Golden Flame.

"Delightful in memory were our walks, our talks; faithful was he and obedient in the crucibles. Even there, as in Samos, I told him of you, Pensatia, and that you would meet in the land of the Eagle, there in the West where mountains soar high. Yes, I instilled the vision of you, your work, that he might be called to his role. Yes, Masters know things to come, and that which is. Yet even as I did fall, as you know, in this life he almost at the peak of attainment did succumb to the Black Art; their unholy rites deluded him from his esoteric light. He denied me, calling me impostor; he became head of the most benighted cult, and even to this day pays his karma for such. Yet let me say, in bringing forth my words penned through Pensatia, he shall liberate in full his betrayal. Remember all who seek the Way, to renounce a true Master bears heavy Karma indeed. Yet be it known, never again will he betray the Light. He again is at my heart's altar. Yes, Pensatia, it was you who moved him from the Path; even so it is you who in this life opens the way (as Saul of Tarsus) for you both to make reparation. Let me say this, in incarnations after, you two served the Masters and the Path in beautiful oneness together as even today you will. For through the suffering and sorrow of that one incarnation, you both learned for good, that only love of soul and heart for the Rose Immortal matters; all else is vain. Yet in remembering that, let not austerity disbar humanity and the forming of ties in this life, for I have forgiven, forgotten, even as my Guru forgave me.

"Thus it is, Pensatia, we weave our self-made destiny together. Thus it is we must unweave negation, into love and beauty and service to God and the Masters. Yes, at the close of that fated life in India, you both came and asked for my forgiveness and together we did sip on the Holy Mountain. We partook of the Lord's Supper and there you two were wed and all the infamous rites of the Black Art you exterminated and did start afresh, knowing me for the true Guru that I was, though poor, without worldly goods; I aided you, cosmic strength was given to build anew. Death claimed you both in old age; I saw your ashes sown upon the foot hills, and there today if you were to travel a memory would be awakened. Yes, strange and wonderful are the windings of one's journey on the Wheel of Life. Today you work in unity for the light; you will find peace and fulfillment and see the New Age flower. So it is written. Even so will all given by me see many lands and tongues; money and the way to publish will come. I speak of this to reveal nothing is by chance and that all inevitably leads to the Master Path."

The Master paused. Silence came upon the rolling cosmic hills, amber haze fell upon the land, and Peace Profound rested true within my heart.

"Pensatia," spoke he, " 'not by bread alone' is a Master made, but by the spiritual intake of cosmic good. Before I attained the signature of the Hierarchal mark, I had to learn to let go of all earthly props, to rely on the spiritual in everything; that is, I had to climb to the Golden Flame and there abide; and even when the Dark Night rolled down upon me, I sipped of the Holy Grail and lifted myself to the garden of the Gods and did eat the food of Isis and drank from the magic well. 'Not my will but Thine be done' I spoke the word for Life, Light and Love, and doubted not, and lo, always supply full and running over came, and health, and my path cleared. I knew Heaven food and earth were one, each contained in the other.

"So, incognito, in one incarnation I walked with royalty and did much to change history. In another I played a part on the Appian Way, and in great Lincoln's day I overshadowed him and aided him to serve his mighty cosmic role. It was karmic cause and effect—his death—he knew it had to come; he was an initiate incognito and though laden with heavy self-made karma, he valiantly obeyed and fulfilled his mission. Soon he reincarnates and plays a leader's part in the coming age. I was with Washington at Valley Forge; I caused the vision of what is to be to come to him. Aye, I have used my Master Staff life after life when needed. Alone and yet a part of all, young, yet old in the ageless regeneration I live today. I come in many guises to my trusted disciples. I am ever near, even as now I overshadow the Defender of the Rose. He is to walk the Path again and know even now regeneration has begun. I shall never leave his side, night or day, until his weakness turns to strength. He will paint and teach as never before. So I have spoken, so it will be. Farewell, Pensatia, until another page from my life."

I arose, for my Guru had departed.

chapter ☆☆ SEVEN

I journeyed to meet again Guru Master H. The green grass waved, the cosmic air was soft and oh, so clear. I walked towards him coming from afar; in his hand was held a book. It was black, yet white light and gold sparkled from its binding, and behold, the Christus image flashed upon it. The Master put the book within my hand.

"Behold, Pensatia, the Way, the Rose, the Lotus, aye, the Buddha, Confucius, the Kabbala—all paths are founded in the Christus of the Absolute. All esoteric books in different tongues proclaim the Christ light, the shining Grail. On the Master Path, all the Masters gone before point to the Star of Cosmic Consciousness, the savior of all humanity. O that blessed incarnation when in flesh I walked and learned from Jesus the man, before and after he was Christed—his patient nobility, wisdom. There in the esoteric school, hidden from the masses, he came and taught me under the Judea sun. There by hill, stream and valley I learned the discipline, the initiations of the Essenes. I traveled with the greatest of Avatars.

"Behold, this 'book' contains not only the personal diary of my words, but also, to those able to read therefrom, is given in distress or when needing to know, quick answers; open and ask, it will give true. Open now and ask."

I did take the black book with lustrous light, the book of truth given to all disciples at a certain sounding of the esoteric Gong. I asked, and lo, all white the answer flashed in bold, clear letters.

"Yes, Pensatia, from Akasha is this esoteric record, which in time all initiates learn to read therein; what is asked from the heart, the answer is read, what is read will be. The disciple may ask for others as well—the answer will be given. I give this now to you, Pensatia. Ever keep it within thy heart's consciousness and in the Flame of Gold. Use it, read only what is written within its pages. To some, their earthly mission will be to read for man; if so, obey. Obtain thy earthly license—supply will come. Have no set price; yet large or small, receive what is offered thee. The more in faith one asks from the Sacred Book of Light, the clearer the answer; so in the Flame of Gold hesitate not to read from Akasha. Here the Scroll of Life unfolds, and past, present and future. It is only possible to use this divination in the Gold."

From my heart I answered: May this book be treasured, may power be given to read clear.

"So it will be, Pensatia, obey and even when all seems not, reach up and pen pages from my life's history. Now in this my today, in the pages of Akasha, all is seen, even into the Aquarian age. The Book of Fate, of which Napoleon found the earthly duplicate; Akasha's Book, may it be utilized to turn, to answer all, and to commune with all minds and dimensions from the Cosmic Hierarchy to Hades' realm. Yet remember, only in the Gold may one read from this esoteric book. Often, it is true, those not consciously on the Master Path reach up and attract inspiration from Akasha. But to do so at will in objective awareness one must attain the Golden Flame. In this is the unity of the Finite and Infinite; to live, work and love in it brings forth inevitable regeneration of thy earthly body, and thy body of light comes forth Master; in fact, thy physical temple fuses with the other and creates the Alchemical Marriage. This does not deny earthly mating, but draws the true complement to one, as said before.

"Pensatia, when nausea or weakness comes, stay on; sip of the Gold, imbue the red. It is only the purging of the Gold. Each day in it such symptoms pass; each day, youth, vitality, balance and wisdom will be more. All who come in the presence of they who stand in the Gold will be uplifted, blest, healed in some degree.

"This Book of Fate, black, with its pure white rays, comes to every disciple who attains the Golden Flame and stays in it. Know when this is given one, that which is spoken will be—so ask for others and thyself, but not that which hurts another. Turn the pages with a grateful heart; have patience, live naturally, in the world, yet not of it. Render unto Caesar and unto God, love all, forgive all and know in the Gold thou art whole. Thus is life renewed through all thy being. All outward signs of age will fade, for in the Gold is the Elixir of Life.

"Pensatia, I Master H, have used this physical temple for years beyond the century mark, and today am in the virility and health of a man in his prime; my square beard is iron gray, every gland, organ, artery is vital, even younger than you. My beloved disciples sense me as the personification of the Regenerative Life promised to all students who obey and attain the Golden Flame."

He turned and bored through me with his eyes of Mastership.

"Richard will attain the Waters of Baptism; even now the dross is washed away. Regeneration will be. A great healing takes place. A master teacher of esoteric wisdom comes forth, even so, a master painter. I have spoken from the Book of Fate. Even so will Virgo of the Incas come to the Rose, and she of days gone by will liquidate their karma, and the 'Fish' (Pisces) shall leave all, and the love that was, will bear again—before Xmas' Holy Night, a union immortal will be. I have spoken, so be it; and to all who read, seek and obey—the way will open to meet me. My blessing now is upon you. Arise and enter the Path. The Gold is the harvest of the Way, the integration of the all, the diploma given one to stand and be in cosmic consciousness. Such, Pensatia, is the law. Be faithful in thy Gethsemane and even so will all walk forth in the Golden Flame to do and dare in God's Holy name, the Word which ever glows in the Gold. So it behooves mankind to seek and enter the Master Path; thus only will the Holy Grail be his.

"Thus life after life I pressed on. The crucible purged and made me tempered steel. On every spiral, I braved the Dark Night of the Soul and breathed anew the Golden Dawn. I liberated my self-made cause and effect. Little by little I earned my Master Signature. Now I wear the Rose in bloom upon my heart, the song of life flows through me. All tongues I speak. I stand afar, yet near, hearing and reading the hearts of men. Those ready find me, those seeking, I overshadow; if they persevere, they too know me. I aid over and through all objective barriers; my love touches all humanity, even those who know me not. Even so is the Defender overshadowed, even so does supply come.

"Have faith, Pensatia; these my words, pages from my journeys on the Path, and all given you by me, you will live to see in the printed book. Even so will the way clear for such to be. So it is spoken; so will it be."

Thus closes the seventh chapter.

The Guru walked away. I felt the twilight of earth far below, heard the echo of the Master's words: "Obey, Pensatia, thou art cared for, heaped up and running over . . ."

chapter ☆☆ **EIGHT**

There in the rosy dawn of fourth dimensional meadow Master H greeted me. "Pensatia, easy does it on the Master Path," said he. "A steady application to cosmic consciousness is required. My Guru, he who lives in Alaska, labored with me for one whole incarnation before I attained the Golden Star of Love. Yes, even though I had climbed to occult power and high honors, still I had not awakened to love, and to feel the heart oneness with all life. My occult credentials were taken from me. I was stript bare— all was swept away. Like a neophyte, I started again to realize that all occult powers without love and compassion for humanity were empty glory and would only lead to a dead end. Only that which is spawned from soul truly lives —so I was set back again. All manner of humanity, from high to low, crossed my path. In humble obedience to the Rosy Path, the full love vibration was awakened within my heart, and lo, its beam was turned upon all I met. I realized that all was love—in man, beast and plant. It took one whole incarnation of steady perseverance to become conscious of such; it was only my preceding foundation that made even this possible. Yet a few of my disciples will learn in shorter time. Such is the law—application and obedience alone count. . . .

"In the penning of this book and those before many will ask: Who is Master H? I Master H have borne many names through the ages. My name matters not; it is what the message bears—it alone holds the signature of what I am. Thus, Pensatia, say to high and low, namely: I am known to you as Master H. If I bear likeness to any of the known Masters, so be it; I neither confirm nor deny. Master H is the name I use in this incarnation. Heed my words, not my *nom de plume*. Let me be known rather as Brother Servant of the Holy Grail. That I was known to Marie Corelli—even to those who deny my words—that I overshadowed as Friend, Alden, when the Rose again bloomed in America; that even today I watch and see the workings of the Rose. I speak in fact. All the Masters are Brothers in one cause: to serve God the Creator and to aid cosmic consciousness in man.

"Heed my message, take the Path—enter and obey—follow the crucibles and I, or another, will surely come as Master to lead one through Rose and Cross to the Holy Grail. Such is he who will see to the publishing of all received by you, Pensatia; he will know me yet in fullness. Even so will the Rose bear witness to this and all gone before and what will come after. So speaks the Word. My work is world-wide, yet with ease I now perform my mission. I come in many guises to my disciples and disciples-to-be. Some will know me as Master H, even as does Pensatia. To others I will come in different ways and other names; it matters not, only that I come. Ageless, without time, I walk the earth where and when I will. I speak the

Word and *it is* in fiat of Cosmic order. I share and know
the heart sorrows of the world and man, yet see beyond
and know this too will pass. I have lived in Dante's Hell;
now in consciousness I wield the Master Staff. And I say
now unto you, Pensatia, and to all who walk the Path,
what is spoken in my heart for you, will be. . . .

"In that incarnation I learned the simple life, that of
herb, garden and stream. I lived by the road and was a
friend to man. Again, I was given the Robe of Mastery
and full cosmic powers, this time spawned by love alone.
Mighty with wisdom from the Father's Heart, I walked
out into life with nothing save faith and my cosmic Robe.
Behold, all the riches of Heaven and earth were loaned me
from cosmic vault for my needs and to serve others. I lived
beyond the century mark and was known as Brother Ben.
Yet even then, as now, I was labeled in Hierarchical Circles, the White Brotherhood esoteric, as Master H. O
blessed is that Holy moment, that life when, weave by weave
one creates the seamless robe, then one steps forth knowing
all is love. Only then does the hush of infinite reverence
make most humble the heart and mind for the great privilege of the ancient mystical Path leading to the Holy
Grail. I passed through the mystery of transition, yet was
beyond it, even as Alden and all Avatars and Masters.
They assume often death's guise, often to challenge the
disciple's faith. Yet a few see into the mystery, and know
they never died, even as Jesus the Christ. Behold, O disciples, ponder on this. Yet in that incarnation the lowly,
the rich, outcasts, came to my funeral rites. I, known as
Brother Ben, was loved and mourned in the green valleys
and far in the cities of man, and the earth carried my love
vibrations near and far. I Master H had only taken on
another assignment, another cloak. Even now if one re-
searched back, they would unearth records of Brother Ben.

"In the following role of life's arena, much power was
mine, in the circle of the so-called elite, the moneyed few,

the intelligentsia. I lived among them incognito, a man of great wealth, having the respect and love of aristocrat and commoner alike. There I drew a treasured few disciples upon the esoteric path. There in the most worldly atmosphere I used my inner power, my riches, to good and noble use. All were welcome at my estate or manor house. There on the esoteric Thursday eve, weekly I and the hierarchal Masters met and outflowed strength and aid to humanity.

"So you see, Pensatia, life after life the student starts, obeys. Then one steps forth in consciousness with the God of all people; the Christus has come forth in most Holy White to heal and to bless; henceforth, in the world and not of it. Every true Master in relative degree is a way shower of cosmic light. They overshadow the lesser to bring forth the greater. They mate with Heaven, even as they mate with earth. Synthesizing all things, love is their essence, their wand of magic. They have lived all notes of life, bathed in all waters; integrated, they behold the inner signature of all things. What a task! Often thankless, often crucified, often obeying strange and secret missions. Yet ever with peace within, they have the joy of the illuminated heart, the presence of the Holy Grail, through the doubts, fears, sorrows of the Cross. They have triumphed; now with loving understanding they carry a part of their disciples' cross, ever easing when karmicly possible the Dark Night of the Soul. O weary ones who have entered the Holy sacred night, give not up at thy dark hour, know in the shadows the Masters stand and watch. Keep faith, we see, know and understand your weakness, karma, your needs; obey even when Gethsemane comes, when health seems not. I say this will pass. In the Light, the disciple transmutes the lesser into the higher, and in the meeting of the two a higher dimension comes to birth."

The Master turned and looked upon the waving grass of Heaven land. "As waving as these ripples from cosmic

wind, so all life on earth is vibrational; constant change
walks the Maya's realm. Yet within man's heart, Pensatia,
is a still and Holy calm which no outer storm can rend.
Seek that, O man, for there only is the Shekinah of thy
divinity. Dare, do and be silent save to heal, bless and
love; such is God's inevitable law. Law and order, cause
and effect, and within, Peace Profound. Such is the Mecca
of mankind's search.

"Back of the sun of earth flows the Gold of the Absolute
down through man and earth, mixing the twain and forming the marriage of the infinite and finite, thus proclaiming
the cosmic mandate: as above so below, as below so above.
Only as man becomes conscious that all is one does he
obtain the Elixir and Stone of the Alchemist."

Now the Master's face grew stern and grave beyond the
ken of man, yet compassionate, with eyes holding all
earth's sorrows.

"One whole incarnation was spent studying compar-
ative religion on the Path. I steeped my consciousness in
the great edifices and cathedrals, talked with Catholics,
Protestants, Buddhists, Zoroasterites, Hindus, Yogis. I
worshipped in all dedicated altars. At the close of that
life, I entered and found the Cathedral of the Soul, that
vaulted structure of infinite dimensions. There, and there
only, was found the Vestal Flame which led to Cosmic
Consciousness. Yes, in that life I realized in the Aquarian
age man will learn to first contact and realize the Christus
within. I learned first-hand that God walks and talks
through nature and the stars, that His laws are inevitable,
that all is by Grace; learned that Karma is not harsh, but
most just, that we ourselves weave our own pattern from
divinity.

"So it was, life after life on the Master Path I learned
by initiations in the esoteric crucibles and assignments of
my Guru. I earned the six-pointed seal of the Holy Hexagram and stood beyond the veil of Maya, and read *true*

... life's inner signature. Rising triumphant in the Golden Flame, I equalized body, mind and soul. That one incarnation was Holy Oil to my Mecca, the reward of all my crucibles. O the sweet peace within, that calm which no outer storm can shake, that oneness with the Father. In that life I verily found the Truth, the Holy Grail, the Love which Christs all things, man or beast. Today, Pensatia, I stand apart yet near, am one with all, yet beyond Maya's lure. Draw near me, who seek the Path—we the Masters hear, see and know. For through the Dark Night, the crucibles and wars, we will not fail the sincere student. I say it now with finality, say it with the power of the Word: give not up, though all Maya seeks to tear you from the Path. Keep vigil with faith even when destitute and alone. I promise all—yes, we the Masters of the Esoteric Path— even at the last moment, if obedient, you shall not want; if faithful, even thy karmic prison I will lift, and lead you to Golden Dawn. I have spoken, Pensatia, aye, repeat this to the Defender. For in the Masters' Hall he is greatly loved; he builds anew and true."

So spoke the Guru, the Master H. "Go back, Pensatia; another day, another time, I will resume these pages from my yesterdays."

chapter ☆☆ NINE

Across the cosmic green came Master H, and behold, riding by, the White Horseman of fabled lore. Even as I looked, horse and rider vanished in cosmic mist. My Guru spoke:

"Always at certain milestones on the Master Path blazes the White Horseman across our path. It is indeed a momentous occasion, for such heralds cosmic consciousness to come. My Guru had told me to prepare and ever watch for the Esoteric Rider. Well do I remember, Pensatia, my first and only glimpse—for seldom does he show himself twice. It is written in records of Akasha: Never does the fabled Horseman show himself until the Walker of the Way has made ground. To see him is to know one is pointed towards illumination . . .

"It was dusk—sitting on the coast of Ireland on its emerald sod, musing on the gold of setting sun; the Path seemed most rugged, heavy with obstacles, unyielding to my mortal self. Doubt crept upon my mind, so futile that evening hour did the cosmic quest seem. Rising I made back to my simple habitation beyond the hill and down in wooded glen. I walked in . . . and by the hearth still red with heat of embers, I sat and pondered on my way to Mastership. It was then, looking up, galloping by came the White Horseman. For a second he turned, eyeing me, and in a flash vanished. Yet in that split second of inner sight granted me, a strange and Holy peace ran through my heart, blood and bone. It was as if God and the Christus touched me. I knew and felt the wonder and grace of the Path; travel I would to journey's end. A quickening took place within my holy centers of perception.

"Yes, Pensatia, and disciples-to-be, ever walk the Path, for you know not when the Esoteric Horseman appears. Persevere and even as I, the Horseman will appear, indicating one's cosmic progress. It was this visitation which encouraged and gave me strength to face the many tasks given me on Irish soil. It was incognito, my life in Ireland among the tinkers, the peasants. I lived alone on the outskirts of the Irish bogs; there, often toiling by day, studying by night in my alchemist shop, and in the silence did wield and create the Philosopher's Stone and Elixir. And there again, I had for esoteric students those two of Gypsy and Inca blood. There, once more love's blossom bloomed and again I wed them, even as today shall they vow the marriage rites, or liquidate the need. So it is written, so will it be.

"It was a blessed incarnation. Despite my arduous mission given me at the close of life, there in secret was wielded the Rose dew. An influx from the Afflatus of the Illuminati seeded the green of Ireland with light which even to this day is seen. Yes, nature and heaven conceived and brought forth a seed which is to blossom into Aquarian age. My Guru from Samos did do me homage, when my body was hoary with a century and more. My beloved students, seven in number, carried me out to the sloping hills, out to earth and its spirits of wood and stream, out where in the silence of the night, in clear conscience my body of light emerged from its temple of clay, and thence came forth a Hierarchal Master. The Defender, who was then an initiate, was bequeathed my earthly orders yet not finished, and well did he take on the task. Studied he deep in the night, the hidden key of the Arts. There, was given him the seeding of his painting today. Yes, out of that past comes the artist immortal today, and the Aquarian age. Faithful he was then to the Alchemy of the Rose; even now he comes forth in this life with his staff, comes he with his cosmic brush. So passed the round of the coming of the Horseman, the initiations and cosmic attainment of the Green Isle.

"Those seven students live scattered here and there now, in different lands. Some have met, others are to meet —yet two will never again know each other; Karma is finished. To he who also was a disciple here in Ireland, he who now will never cease his vigil until all received by Pensatia is published, he will yet know first-hand my touch. To her, let me say, in the Gold is life, health and abundance; fulfillment comes in all phases of life; before autumn ends much comes to pass—across the seas a letter of vast importance; also a complete lifting of physical karma, and a union of the past. Even now this day comes a surprise of magnitude. I inject these personal gleanings from Akasha that all who read may sometime, somewhere realize I speak not falsely. And to all who read in deep sincerity these episodes of my history, be it known to each I will lay a blessing and a realization of a heart desire in this life. So be it, I have spoken.

"To go back. You see, it takes threads from many incarnations to round out a Cosmic Master. From each life on the Master Path, rough spots are chiseled off, and awakenings are brought about, as in some puzzle. In time, a past, present and future fit in and are seeded from many lives. The one cosmic reason for this book is above all else to reveal that the Master Path is a long journey stemming from our yesterdays and transcending into our future, until is born the realization—*all is one*. When one has arrived, remember, the Master Cape, the Staff, must ever bear witness to life, light and love. My Staff of Authority I use wherever I go, my Cape is ever about me. I walk city streets and country lanes, having many abiding places—I assume many characters. Many pass me by, even my disciples, never knowing I was the person perhaps who knocked at their door, the man who passed them on the streets. Often I assume the guise of a derelict from Skid Row, that I might discover master timber or watch how my students act toward their fellow man. Yes, I walk in all places, among all people. I shall live long in this incarnation, beyond the 144 cycle; I shall walk and wield my Master Staff, even as other Masters, even as the Tibetan, that infallible Light of Cosmic Hierarchy. Often there in the high Himalayas, under the pine of the Master Jesus, we gather in conclave and partake of Holy Communion, and bread and wine of the Holy Supper. There we renew ourselves and bathe in the immortal waters which give regeneration. Rising in the Golden Flame, we ever fuse the green essence of earth with the gold of Heaven. Hence, disciples of the Path, when you attain the knowledge to walk in this Flame of Gold, never leave it, partake of all earthly things, yet ever in the Gold. For the Gold regenerates and stabilizes positive and negative; it gives one the power to speak the Word and bring forth.

"According to Divine Will, I come into the hearts of those ready for me; then, as they rise in consciousness and obedience, we the Masters make ourselves seen inwardly. We watch and guide those on the Path to the Holy Grail; our earthly wants are externalized as we need; even so it is with our disciples. Never does God or the Masters fail them on the Path in their Hour of want. Ever is their negative karma softened by the Masters' love and their obedience. Often, time seems to enter in—that which is spoken by the Master often appears void of realization. But mark well my words, never does the Master speak without results. Sometimes disciples misinterpret our words; that is because their personal emotion enters in. Only when the disciple learns detachment does he hear true the Master's words. That is, one must learn to listen only to the Guru, even if at times he denies one. Many and many a time did my Guru relate from Akasha or from the Jade Tablets. That which was written often took years before coming to pass; at other times, instant fulfillment was. Often after days or months, suddenly out of the blue, comes what was spoken. Ever will it be, Pensatia, with all disciples of the Way who are obedient and brave the crucibles. It seems I give at random the many parts that made my Mastership, yet law and order runs through the puzzle. All fit in, though often it seems a paradox; often related happenings come far between, seemingly unrelated; yet nothing happens by chance. All incarnations in cosmic eye are woven together—cause and effect—though effect follows often many lives after, or at once. So if all in this book appears not in so-called sequence, know all dovetails in my cosmic pattern, like a giant puzzle. As one attains cosmic consciousness, one sees the mystery cleared; often the first is last and the last first. So in these my lives, seek first the message, the esoteric code rather than the letter, for unless you are aware of the meaning of the Master's voice behind my book, it is in vain one reads it."

Now the veil of matter fell over the Heaven meadows. Master H did depart, yet the glory of his presence trailed with me back to earth.

chapter ☆☆ **TEN**

It seemed long I sat beneath a sprawling tree in Akashic meadows green. At last, slowly approaching with Staff, came venerable Master H. I rose to greet him, my beloved Guru.

"Relax here, Pensatia, while from memory's hall I relate points from the great All.

"I climbed high to the Mountain of the Gods—to the Sinai of illumination, and lo, brought to mankind, as all must, that revealed in the Fire of Isis, the burning bush of Cosmic Consciousness. All who return shine with the glory of their Holy Orders and the Light granted them. Never again are they the same. They walk the earth crowned with their illumination. It is a heavy privilege, a cosmic responsibility which sets them apart from their old life; that is, a new quality is added which often creates a vast loneliness. Exemplifying the light makes one conscious of earth karma and those still in the valley of ignorance. The Master, adepts, disciples, speak a common tongue, yet only a few share the esoteric dimension. Experienced, he hears the music of the spheres, communes with nature's heart, which obeys his will. He has attained, yet is a

brother to all men—unrecognized often, for man causes
a barrier which keeps Master and pupil apart. Thus the
Master's heart is sad; for man must make the first step forward. Alas, so very few make it! Why, oh why, you ask,
Pensatia? Karma, taking the line of least resistance, a closed
mind—all these are barriers. Then, too, fears enter in.
They dare not the way to the pearl of great price. No
Master may break the self-made wall to the Path. Man
himself, with dedicated heart, must answer the call to cosmic consciousness. There is a most high price attached to
Mastership; few are willing to pay it. As reported in all
occult books, again and again is the mandate: All must
drink the cup of the Cross, all must experience the crucifixion, brave the crucibles, and work to make gold in the
alchemist shop. None can evade the Dark Night of the
Soul. Yet to those who obey inevitably comes the tran-
scendental cosmic consciousness.

"In this tenth chapter, Pensatia, I disclose a lonely road.
Traveled I heavy with earth sorrows. How I longed to get
away from it all—my mission, all my illumination seemed
as naught. Ah, student of the Rose, all Masters again and
again are faced with this yearning; yet remember, if faithful it passes ere it comes. So it was with me. Taking my
Staff and making way to the desert, to the sands of the
Gobi, there under the cool of night and the upward blue
of a thousand stars, I pondered on my journey through
many lives on the Path. Weary I was at the slow pace of
humanity. Memories of Maya's colorful panorama, the
music of earth, seemed so dear to me, and the Master role
seemed too heavy. I knew I was to be given a new assignment soon, the most arduous yet. Danger, aye, life itself
might be asked, the parting from my beloved wife. Was I
strong and big enough to renounce everything again, just
when the Father had given me the all? Forty days and
nights I sank—body, heart and mind—there on desert
sands, growing gaunt from my vigil, from the struggle.

Yes, Pensatia, in that life when aware of the Master's Cape, still there was a dragon to be slain. There always is when one is close to the Magi's crown. Knowing as all disciples know, that drinking of the bitter cup of the crucifixion by the multitude must come; though innocent and working only for humanity, there assuredly comes that incarnation when one is stoned, for the very light. I had the power to avenge and destroy those who sought to tear me apart. It is then, even as Jesus, one must cry out, 'Not my will but Thine.' When this inevitable cry is heard and the disciple obeys and drinks the bitter cup of crucifixion, one arises with new power, a cosmic peace descends. In silence, he faces his sad yet glorious destiny, going forth to face the stoning. All in relative degree in some incarnation must face this; only the promise of the resurrection and the presence of my Guru's face gave me strength to tighten my cordelia and go forth and meet my Gethsemane. Yes, I—we, all the Masters who attain—must in some life be crucified for the light we bear. Yet in vain the wanton ignorance, the stoning, the negation of the Rose of Life. Behold, its splendor is greater than all martyrdom, the Cross. Behold, it is then the Master steps forth in such illumined brightness no tomb can hold him. It is finished. With the Christus the disciple comes forth a Master of love, wisdom and illuminated consciousness.

"Yes, Pensatia, back in my yesterdays—back in the days of Cromwell—innocent though I was, working only for the Master Hierarchy, I was pulled across the public market place, denounced as a Demonic Wizard, a charlatan. Yes, I was burned at the stake. Yet, behold, my Guru Master did stand in the flame and it touched me not. The 'Veil of the Prophets' prevailed and I escaped with my Guru. When the mist cleared, the mob saw only the dying embers and assumed it was my cremation. Thus do the Masters of the White Lodge save the faithful disciple, those who are given the cosmic role. Thus, Pensatia, did I pass the fire of crucifixion and afterwards did make my way to the hills of Lebanon, and there among the pines I did use my body of light to germinate the Rosy seed. I did go to all points of the compass, traveling as the wind. I gathered my disciples close to my heart's Shekinah, and they heard and obeyed, and great in that life was the awakening of their centers of light. And I mapped my course for this incarnation now. Though free from the astrological Wheel of Birth, by free choice and desire of my blessed Guru, I took upon me the cape of this Age. You, Pensatia, the Defender, aye, he who shall bring forth all written through you, were, are and will be my valiant disciples who will attain, even as all who read and dare the crucibles and disciplines of the Way.

"With this retelling from my many lives on the Master Path, much may seem at times like a great puzzle. Yet related to the whole are these pages. I wish to convey to the reader that most Holy order of the Way, and that many bricks must be laid firm and soundly cemented by obedience and doing.

"Only after the stoning and crucifixion comes the free play of all one's cosmic mission. All the Avatars, after the martyrdom, lived in their body of light, ascended Masters walking the earth incognito, teaching, aiding and bringing forth the Word in world affairs. In this Age I sense the coming trends, know and work with the Cosmic Hierarchy. With all planets I have close intercourse. With the Venusians and Martians, the Jupiterians, and from the Saturnian Lords of Karma I read and give to my worthy students when ready, knowledge that will aid them.

"The Defender, if faithful, shall in flesh visit me here and attain the most high initiation. Even so you, Pensatia, if you pass the higher disciplines and sip of the white water; even so he my disciple of other days. Yes, I have taken you and others through many initiations. I who have been through Dante's Hell and won, share my grace, my vic-

tory with you, my students and disciples-to-be. I quicken
your centers when ready and lift your consciousness to
higher levels and give you fourth dimensional food and
drink. As the Master becomes, so must he give back, teach
or initiate those chosen to discipleship. I have been in all
the States of the U. S. A. In the years ahead, and beyond
in the 20th century I shall, with Master St.-Germain and
the Tibetan, be in conclave, and we three shall often stand
in the shadow in government and congress. A high Master
Initiate soon comes forth and appears as common man
among the people. And a woman of the people will do
much to aid him. I have spoken. The Word declares. It
will be. A vast rebirth of the Atlanteans floods the earth.
Many Venusians come at the Masters' call. Sex will be
known in its spiritual impact in the years ahead. Women
and men who desecrate the creative function and barter in
flesh shall be taken from life.

"I live in many places, still using my earthly body,
which is regenerated by the Flame of Gold. I shall use it
on into the new century. Then shall be revealed my full
cosmic name, and a great mystery shall be solved. For even
now the greatest upon the Path are not sure who and what
I am. Bear this in mind, Pensatia, you who know me as
Master H only—though too, you recognize me by another
name: Heliobas. There is a place, a quiet glen, a wayside
house high on a mountain slope of Tibet, far from the rush
of life, still untouched by ravishers. There, when ready,
I bring psychically or in flesh my disciples. There I en-
gender the rest, healing and stamina needed to bring forth
the Rose in bloom. There one embraces the Golden Flame
and learns to equalize all things. There weekly or daily I
bring my disciples and attune them to the fourth dimensional altitude. Some—a few—tarry long here; they long
to stay in this Shangri-La of learning. Here no earth
duality reaches them—only the purity of the Path, the
white light nested in Golden Flame. Here they sup and live

in the aura of the Hierarchical Masters of the White Brotherhood who meet here and initiate the disciples called.

"For we are fast coming into the Christus period, when all life shall express the cosmic mandate—as above so below, as below so above. Hence all who are on the Master Path, slowly, steadily obey day by day, build thy body of light, so that you may regenerate and walk into the new age of cosmic consciousness. It can be if you will work and fulfill the Way. You who have slipped back into Maya's unreality, turn now, and even as you do in sincerity, so will I and all the Masters aid you. The first shall be the last, and the last first.

"It is thus I write this account of my Cosmic Journey, that you might know the mercy of God and the Masters. As I made the mountain top, so can and will all humanity in the New Age. Do not think we Masters do not enjoy mundane living. We enjoy with far more relish than the non-Master; we have learned use but not abuse is the law. Mastered have we the disciplines, transmuted in the crucibles, and made gold in the alchemical shop; we are free to enjoy all phases of earth life, not dependent on them. We partake or not, as the occasion demands. All scales of life we have Christed, though in the world we are not of it. We see all in the whole, we have borne witness to the Alchemical Marriage, hence are ready for our complement outwardly in woman. We may partake of flesh, fowl or fish, plant, herb or vegetable, for in love all nature serves us, and we give back to nature. Yet in Mastery we sip of all life, yet abuse naught. Thus it is not by revolution we aid our pupils, but by evolution and self-mastery, exemplified by the Living Rose upon our hearts. Some of my disciples, who have earned the right, I walk and talk with. I meet them in cosmic dimensions and reveal through pen and canvas, music or the healing arts, cosmic wisdom. We open Akasha's most sacred books and enable the student to read, to see, to know the wonders of the White Brotherhood. We overshadow, bring aid when sleeping and rejuvenate the physical body. My chief habitat is high, near the lone pine of the Himalayas—there where the Master Jesus presides over the Last Supper and the Holy Grail, there where in groups of 12 the disciples of the Path come and take Holy Communion, and Jesus in some manner speaks to each. Also I speak and teach in the clear mountain air my disciples able to contact me. My physical body is free of dross. Every cell, gland and organ is regenerated into its cosmic purity. When I leave my body for good, I the Master, simply walk from it and ascend to the Inner Brotherhood. What is left of my outer body disintegrates at once; even so it is with all who attain Mastership. No one becomes a full Master until they prove themselves in all ways.

"Yes, Pensatia, now as I view all lives as a whole, as I relate parts of my journey to Mastership, I speak with one voice with all the Masters. A Master is made only by obedience, and treading the Path through all obstacles, joy and sorrow, loss or gain. A Master is made by creating within himself or becoming aware of the 12 ingredients which bring forth the Stone and Elixir. A Master in the making must pour himself as a dedicated sacrifice to God and the Cosmic. In some incarnation in one full sweep all must be discarded for the Quest of the Holy Grail. One must, as Jacob Boehme, have only one love, to find the inner signature of nature and man. There is that hour, that incarnation when the disciple bursts full bloom into the heart of the Father. In that life, know Pensatia, in full consciousness the Master emerges, like a butterfly from its chrysalis. It is for this incarnation all students, disciples and initiates work. This can come in any life. In the Akashic records the gong sounds out when the Master comes forth."

The Master H turned, his face lighted up like the sun.

"Pensatia, there is nothing mundane—word or otherwise
—that can do justice to that joy when one realizes his full
oneness with the Father, nature and man. For this are the
journeys of life on earth, for this does man bear the crucibles and carry his Cross up Golgotha Hill. For this does
he let go for a moment of the lesser, only to find the
whole. For this does the neophyte take the Path with holy
vows, to find the Holy Grail, the Elixir and the Philosopher's Stone. In writing episodes from my pilgrimage, I
look back and bless every step of the Way, through fog,
mire and sorrow and pain, through the long Dark Night;
I kiss the Rosary and bless the Cross."

He, Master H, drew his cape about him and his golden
aura lighted the Heaven meadow, and lo, the white birds
of Heaven flew low about him and a thousand and one
flowers most holy blue and yellow bright bloomed from
the green grass, and the music of the spheres rolled
through the cosmic meadow. The benediction of Allah,
God, the Christus, crowned my beloved Guru with the
signature of the Holy Grail. My eyes, my heart were awed
and humbled by the cosmic brightness, and all the tears
of earth and Heaven poured through this man who had
made his way to the mountain top. And now a hush fell
upon the cosmic dimensions—amber haze, soft like candle-
light covered all. My Guru stepped away. "Peace, Pensatia, go back to mundane habitat. Closed is this tenth
chapter."

chapter ☆☆ ELEVEN

"These final chapters I would share most closely with
my disciples and those-to-be and with all who seek to place
their feet on the outer path. When reading, center thy

consciousness in the heart and listen. Everything is mathematical law and order. If man fulfills the master formula, a Master comes forth; there is no digressing or evading the cosmic mandate: as above so below, as below so above. One must attain from within and then out. There is no other way.

"In all my many lives the sum total dovetails from every experience, cause and effect being the master manipulator, claiming its just due ere one could progress. I learned, as all must learn, that a firm foundation must precede cosmic attainment. Now having been purged in the crucibles, having braved earth, air, fire and water initiations, having by Grace—which is a higher equation—earned my Master Cape and the Holy Staff, I am at home in all lands, all races, rich or poor. I have the use of money, jewels of earth and heaven when needed. I speak the Word—it is. Yet remember, I am only custodian of cosmic powers. Remember also, only when soul growth comes first—*then only* are occult powers lasting. All else is spurious and is taken away—only that which sprouts from the heart is eternal.

"In this eleventh chapter I would say again, the tempter, those of the Black Brotherhood, even at the last round of cosmic ladder ever seek to destroy the disciple, the adept. Even a Master—until grounded on the mountain top with the signature of the Holy Grail—may be tempted and even succumb. Yet know, having weathered all phases of the Master Path, now in peace profound I walk the earth; in cities, valleys, mountains, I come to those whose light glows in Hierarchical records or Akasha's book. These are tethered under my wings, or other Master's tutelage. Those closest on my round of incarnation gravitate to me. At once is started a subtle consciousness of my presence, which as the student progresses blossoms into that eternal blessing of Master and disciple. At various milestones, I meet with my disciples, often assuming roles incognito.

They know me perhaps as a stranger, or as one interested in their work. Sometimes a trip is made possible. Any character of my many lives I could assume.

"Thus it is, a Master is a man of many cycles blended with the white of cosmic consciousness. I live in the All, drinking as of one cup from all faucets of earth and heaven, experiencing all of the lesser emotions, having mastered and transmuted all; compassion and understanding is ours for those just started or not yet on the Path. Often what I say to my disciples seems paradoxical. Often I speak bluntly, sometimes appear harsh. Yet always remember, no matter in what guise, my love abounds for each and every one of my disciples and disciples-to-be. I do not lack the courage to speak and give to each what the pupil needs. So remember, in thy disciplines and crucibles, students of Rose and Lotus, the least to the most is important; neglect nothing which I give. If one does not catch my small directions, never can one hear the higher orders.

"Hence, Pensatia, all my writings are of equal value, the first and the last. If one is published, even so must all. So speak I Master H. You, Pensatia, shall live to see thusly and beyond. Some things spoken are delayed in coming to pass because of negative karma; rarely one must wait for fruition in another life. Those who have attained the Golden Flame will reap in their present incarnation. Even so will it be for the Defender if he seeks first his Guru's face. Sometimes, even as it was with me, a deep longing is denied until late in life; almost it seems hopeless. But remember, if you ask the Father, Christ or through the Masters, from the heart, it must come to pass. So in this latest incarnation did mine become a reality. O blessed promise of my Guru! blessed fulfillment! Remember, the Masters know your sorrows, your dreams, your hopes, know all you have let go of, your pain. Yet hear my voice —this will pass and joy and peace beyond comparison will be.

"From Akasha I read and study the karma and divine missions of all my disciples-to-be. Even as I see the seed and blossom of the Aquarian age. I soften, manipulate and leaven the sorrows and hopes of man; I stand apart yet close, so close to all. I Master H am known by many names and yet only one, in this life. I have my consciousness in the service of the White Brethren and Cosmic Hierarchy, and above all to the God of all people. When necessary I can bring supply, food, or travel instantly; otherwise I use earth laws. When the cosmic gong sounds for those my students, only then I hasten their desires objectively. We prefer to work with earth laws, yet are able to utilize the super laws, but only for good. As one raises one's vibrations through the Master Path, one is learning to survive and live in the Aquarian age. The law of the cosmos is: learn or perish—awake or degenerate. The disciples of today must acquire that delicate balance of positive and negative and be able to give out the synthesis of Mastership in active service to humanity. No subjective awareness is enough in this new age we are entering. Initiation must be followed by activity in one's cosmic mission. The training of such disciples is the work of the Masters. All my many lives have been a tuning fork for my role as Guru. When students make the grade, that is, attain the Holy Grail and the Stone and Elixir, all Masters rejoice. Until then the Masters, with patience and cosmic wisdom, stand by watching, aiding, teaching and guiding the sincere students through their initiations.

"Pensatia, I feel with and for my disciples. Always when supply seems not, when appearances or karma bring sorrow or pain, I seek to lift and erase the cause, and like a miracle, the disciple finds health, wealth and love coming to pass. I speak in the silence of attunement, in meditation or in intuitional flashes. I often tell my students that which is or will be. I answer questions. One should write down my directions, my words, always, even though they seem false—my message, never doubt, always will come to pass in God's time. The bridge of Akasha I walk at will. In the Cosmic Hierarchy I sit with the Venerables, those infallible Masters of the White Lodge. Daily we scan the work and actions of the disciples. There we give out Holy orders and lift up those who have been brought low.

"Yes, Pensatia, I and all the Masters of this World and higher dimensions walk among you, Brothers of the Third Degree. We never force; with patience we await your feet upon the Master Path. It is then, after probation, we take the disciples-to-be under our tutelage. Thus it is we work eternally to lift man from his self-made ignorance. Every Master has his interludes of enjoying all attributes of earth, when Mastership is his. As the Father states, to lose all is to gain all, of heaven and earth. Yes, often incognito I assume earthly roles; that is, I come among the people as one of them. I often walk in so-called Skid Row to seek therein one ready to hear my voice. I stir, ignite, plant a seed. When a Master walks among, or close, incognito or otherwise, he leaves his stamp upon those ready to enter the Path. Later, or perhaps when they have reached conscious attunement with me, I recall to them when I first met them.

"I shall leave my body in full health and consciousness, and live to beyond the century mark by 40 odd years. I have an assignment yet to carry out. I give back in fortune to my disciple that given to me so long ago. Remember also, I bring to pass a closer bond between two of my disciples and help to bring the Guru to the Defender. Also I see that all my works through Pensatia are published and all kept in circulation. I stay in humble quarters; when needful, in the finest hotels. Often I center in the quiet countryside, yet whenever I wish I can consciously contact my disciples anywhere, at any time, and they me. All things pass before my inner eye. When faith ebbs low and it seems all is naught, it is then I heal and lift up, give

strength and light. Even so, you who read, aye, you, Pensatia, who write my words, ask now and it will be. So be
it—thrice I say—whatever you asked, it now is; behold
with thy soul and know. Thus closes the eleventh chapter
of this History of my lives."

chapter ☆ TWELVE

"I Master H sit now in cosmic meadow and relate
through Pensatia this closing chapter out of my saga on
the Master Path. In that rapport, between Guru and pupil,
may you listen and pen.

"May all who read rise and seek the Way to Cosmic
Consciousness. This is God's design for man. Only when
we realize the first step must begin with us, is one ready
for the Holy Pilgrimage. All outer attributes are as nothing in the Father's eye—only the naked sincerity of the
seeker reaching within. *They only* are sure to find the Path
and their Guru. It is simple—the mandate—love all, forgive all and learn from nature. Walk slowly the middle
path. Even when all earthly props fall away, 'trust God,
see all nor be afraid.' Know there in that Holy hour, inner
communion comes with the All, peace profound, cosmic
consciousness. It is then the disciple, the adept, steps forth
knowing all is one, a divine whole from the Creator's heart.

"In relating a few of my experiences in my many lives,
it is to point out the vast tutelage it takes to bring forth
the Master. To see and sense the Masters, the ignorant
would assume it luck, a special gift this power, and go their
way disgruntled, thinking God favors some and deals out
the opposite to others. Poor self-deluded prisoners of their
divinity! Only as they face the Self within and realize

nothing comes unless earned, from one life to another, Mastership or otherwise, is there hope for their liberation.

"Remember, God is Love—compassion universal. As the prodigal son, one has all gifts of sonship, as one turns from the husks of Maya, and returns to the Father's house, which is full cosmic consciousness. All is forgiven, and the riches of the finished kingdom are his. O vain and egotistic man—to think there is any other way except by Rose and Cross or Lotus Bloom, or through the crucibles of the Alchemical Christ. I live now in the cusp of a New Age— the age of awakening. To those ready, I see that the gate opens, and select those who dare and do and can keep silent. I see far back and far ahead, and ever pray that God's grace bless my students and that full Mastership be theirs.

"My venerable Guru, with ageless regeneration, resides in far Alaska; his name matters not; though having attained Mastership I treasure communion with him. Even as my disciples with me, and will after Mastership. Let my students listen and know as they read, the Masters walk toward them only as they walk towards the Masters. All must first in soul consciousness contact the Abode of the Masters before they, by aid of the Guru, travel there in physical body. The latter happens only if one's mission calls for such contact. In the Himalayas, beyond the Lamas, also in South America, invisible to all but the initiated, abide always one or several Masters. Only in and through the Golden Flame can the disciple regenerate his body to carry the Light which will allow one to reach the habitation of the Great Ones. If attaining said privilege of past tutelage, know the way will open—a month, a year, or perhaps only a week is granted one. Yet in that time, full regeneration comes, and illumination. All that the disciple lacks, is. The disciple knows ahead of time if the Master calls him.

"I want to speak again of the Golden Flame, as it is

the crescendo of the Path. It is that which bridges the gap between the physical and the spiritual and unifies them into a whole. It is the healer of all illness, all lack—the very bones, arteries, glands, organs are rejuvenated and made immortal, young. Even though it appears the opposite, stay in the Golden Flame; know it is doing its regenerating work. In time, all negative symptoms are illuminated into radiant wholeness of body; only one who has passed the cleavage of the centers is ready to abide in the cosmic Flame of Gold. All mundane values are lifted up into their divinity of expression. Early or late on the Path one may have 'orders' to enter the Flame. In the early stages one may seem weak or ill; this is the purging of the Gold, illuminating karmic dross, that regeneration of body become the lighted temple of the soul.

"Pensatia, in this closing chapter, I desire to come close to each reader and in some manner touch their lives, that they may seek the Path and their Guru. Yes, I will bless those sincere seekers and quicken their urge to discipleship. There will be one or several who will walk the Way of Rose and Cross to cosmic consciousness. Yet many will pass by the open door; they also will I bless, knowing in some incarnation they too will walk the age-old Path of the Masters.

"Even as I have attained, even so may every dedicated neophyte now standing midway between heaven and earth, walk in the clearness of the whole. The birth chart and cosmic desire of all is seen, of they who are my pupils. Ever free choice is theirs to regress in the shadows of illusion; ever I seek to suggest the right choice, and to aid them forward on the Master Path. I rejoice when the students plow through to the finish, the awakening of the holy centers. When disciple and Master live and work in the finished kingdom, the state of grace—they work from the finished pattern, which is the secret of Mastership. In the Akashic records, all is pictured of man's divinity, yet he himself must choose the Path. Often those woven in karmic relationship take the negative decision; thus man himself diverts the fulfillment. Yet the lesson to be learned stands and will be acquired by other contacts. Thus cause and effect wields its influence; thus it is man grows in consciousness beyond karma and duality into the dimensions of grace and effortless living.

"Now the curtain is about to run down on the highlight of my incarnations. Ponder on my message revealed. Some will aspire to discipleship; others will read and still linger on the road to Maya; a few I will call ere they finish this History of pages of my many incarnations. Those called will surely attain cosmic consciousness in this life. I will personally bless all who sincerely study my words. A desire of the heart shall be granted them. In unexpected ways this will come about, and by means you know not of. I grant this that all may experience in some little way the grace of God's laws. Even so, Pensatia, shall a desire be granted you; doubt not, know it is.

"As one progresses on the Master Path, the moment arrives when the highest cosmic laws are yours to use at will. Remember, unless prepared and deserving, these laws will not work. Even the black magicians must learn the formula; yet because they introvert the power they inevitably destroy themselves. For only the pure in heart have the blessing of God's most holy laws. Even those of orthodox faith can draw close, if they have the spirit which contacts them with the essence. Yes, through the Mass, prayer, or just living, the sacred laws work; and behold, ignorant men say: 'Behold, a miracle!' Thus you see by my experiences the Master Path passes through all waters life after life, yet one who puts his hand to the plow and follows through attains cosmic consciousness, or the awakening of the living Christus.

"I close, dear readers, having faith that in this life, so close to the Pyramidal fulfillment, that many if not all who read will continue, or start the Master Path. It will not be easy, as you can see by the saga of my travels. Yet know, as in faith and obedience you start, every treasured promise shall be. May all who read feel and sense my love, and from these glimpses of my pilgrimage be encouraged to go forth and dare and do. So mote it be. We will meet those who dare to seek. So, Pensatia, lay down thy pen. Finished is this book of Master H."

THE FLAME OF WHITE

PRELUDE

I Pensatia, humbly walk into the Flame of White, and in obedience to Love, from the crypt of the Flame of Wisdom, in the year of 1943, pen as I receive.

Open your heart, drink with me from the spiral of infinite flow. Ponder well the interior message given me from the inspiration of the infallible Masters who live in consciousness of the Flame of White.

Let us together thank God for the privilege granted me, for it is not I who write, but the "I Am" of my divinity.

Therefore, by the Seal of the Holy Dove, by the Eye of Akasha, and the Blessed Mary, I Pensatia, a student of the Rose, by the aid of the Master H, promise to write this book.

PENSATIA

Dedicated to all who seek its Holy Essence.

chapter ✩ ONE

Come, readers from all countries, students and disciples of the Rose, let me tell you of the most treasured experience on the Path: The glorious Light of the White Flame.

As I write immersed in it, peace and staying power flows through me. Heart and organs respond to their divine purpose. Love, co-breath of my soul, walks at my side.

Up to the Sanctuary of the Hierarchal Christus, the Flame Itself, I stand in the chalice of circular whiteness. Here, as one learns to stand still and cast aside all earthly garments, one may see. All that is, was and shall be is pictured within it.

All students of the Esoteric Path must attain consciousness in this Flame—seeing, hearing, and then come forth, obeying. All work of the Inner Rose is carried on from here.

"Well done, student," so speaks the Christus to all who enter the coil of white.

These are the words from Master H:

"The Flame of White holds the ever beating heart of Love, the nesting place of the 9th vibration, and the instant creation of all your divine and mortal seeking. It is the vibrating answer to every prayer, the supernal goal of every weary Pilgrim of the Path. All who reach the Flame of White and stand therein shall receive heaven, and earth as well. Thus it is written, and thus it will be.

"Let the whiteness of the light of the Flame cover you by day, and night; you then shall walk through all experiences, alive, healthy, a magi to bless and serve. You shall be fed, clothed, housed with the wealth of heaven and earth also. Wedded to Love, your bridegroom shall be finite and infinite.

"Give not up all who tread the Path, sever not allegiance to Lotus and the Rose. Fall you may, but ever arise

83

and climb up to the answer of Man's eternal quest. As one obeys, so shall one speak and bring forth. Air, Earth, Fire and Water shall obey and serve you. A comforter, a partaker of joy, sorrow, loss or gain; all will be equalized, transmuted in the Flame of White. Animals, life of the wild shall pay thee homage.

"At the shrine of Mastery, the absolute bloom of the Rose comes forth for the disciple. The Christus proclaims it, the Dove of the Heart sounds the gong. Mighty Ra cries: Hail to all who are regenerated in the Flame of White.

"Yes, Pilgrims of the Rose, this Flame of White is the prestige all have earned who enter. It is the end of the painful climb through the darkness of the bleeding discipline. Now the disciple has only to be still, reap and obey, thus penetrating the whiteness with one's inner senses. This is not painful as the preceding trials. For all who enter here have experienced the climactic cleavage of the centers, which gains them entrance into the Flame of White.

"To each in a different way does the cleavage take place. To some it comes with acute swiftness, often under the guise of illness. This climax is as lightning. It strikes swiftly, and in one full stroke breaks asunder the earthly chains of the sacred centers, lifting the disciple into his sublime initiation, while still in the body. If transition occurs, a glorious entrance in conscious illumination comes.

"That a battle must be fought . . . at this stage of development . . . is not denied by the Masters. By prayer, faith and utter reliance on the God of your heart—all will survive the inevitable cleavage, if one's mission calls for such.

"This quick climactic severing of the sacred centers spells quick destiny in the career of the student. He is lifted out of his old axis and is transmuted to a new dimension of being. Here in this high vibrational Flame, one must learn to use the awakened centers in sight, hearing and travel. Only with the utmost guidance from the Masters can one in safety learn to function with power and authority here. This Flame of White is the Inner School, the Inner Circle, of which the arduous foundation of the Path is for. . . . To some the cleavage is not so drastic. Neither is the attainment thereafter so complete. The greater the pain, the greater the gain. This does not imply that only those who suffer may find the Way. It does mean that the more pressure and effort the student gives, the more intense the cleavage—the more beautiful the Cosmic Illumination—and the greater the obligations and service thereafter.

"In the mild severance the psychic centers are opened by the aid of a Master. It seems partiality is shown. Yet not so. This grace comes by past cause and effect. Close contact with the Master has been in some incarnation. So now the disciple reaps the blessing when most needed.

"Remember, when this happens and with ease one passes the cleavage, a threefold obligation to use his powers in unselfish service becomes a must for the student. If he fails to work and learn in the White Flame all opportunity in the next life will be denied him. For cosmic law demands in receiving a spontaneous giving back to humanity.

"Those who by shock and pain bear the cleavage, the Master knows, they have learned that all gifts of heaven are only granted us to give back to others.

"There is a third way of admittance to the Flame. It is by the law of assumption. The Masters look into the records of the Word. They see the mission the pupil is to play in the service of the Rose. They perceive the student has exemplified the life of the Rose, borne the thorns with only love activating his every move. Almost the sacred centers open, but because of one great debt of the past the climactic cleavage cannot take place. It is now that the compassion and forgiveness of the Creator works. As

Christ forgave the penitent thief on the cross, so also does
the Christus and the Masters on occasion, by the compelling vibrations of the pupil's penance, use the law of assumption and have the cleavage take place. By this gracious gesture of the Hierarchy, the disciple, devoid of
pain, walks into the coil of Isis. Henceforth the love of his
pure dedication bears example as, unafraid, he communes
with the Masters and carries out their cosmic orders for
universal service.

"So mark well, three methods only open the inner centers to the White Flame: The painful dynamic way; the
aid of another Master or soul mate; or by the direct inter-
vention of the Master. So sayeth the blood of the Rose.
So sayeth I Master H. So is the Word. Here in the temple,
here within the White Flame, are the glories of creation,
the wisdom of God's heart, the endless library of cosmic
dimensions. The exalted departed await in green pastures
the presence of all students of the Path.

"Let us assume we have made the first baby step into
the Flame of Flames. Let not its brightness frighten you.
Know that it is peaceful and quieting. Its essence strength-
ening, healing and life giving. Just be still and drink in its
whiteness with all thy interior body. Bathe daily in its
white vibration. Listen for the voice of the Master. Obey
what is said no matter how soft the voice . . . and ask what
thy will in the Flame, the Master will answer. Believe no
matter if all seems untrue when earth dimensions are resumed.

"Appearances often disarm the disciple when leaving
the whiteness for the lesser, but remember, it is only the
duality, the tempter saying 'believe not'. Smile, rejoice,
say to all negative thought: begone in the name of Love
and the Rose. Then go about your daily duties knowing
all that transpires within the Flame shall be.

"When least expected, the objective realization will take
place, when God speaks. When you hear 'The Gong has

sounded' know the hour is at hand. Fulfillment, materially and spiritually can come in the twinkling of an eye. Whatever the Master asks of you, start and do; thus will the blessing of the Rose be yours.

"Now, Pensatia, you who pen from the Flame, I close this first chapter with the breath of the Logos sealing it, with the promise that all who seek shall find, and in finding enter, and in entering have."

I walked away from the Flame. Three angels stood by. "Blessings be on all who read," they spoke as one. Thus love encompassed me. Again they spoke: "We are the guardians of the whiteness of heaven. Eternally we live at the entrance of the inner circle in the Flame of White."

All who reach here ever sense the angels three. Thus they know they have trod where no earthly man enters.

chapter ✩✩ TWO

Master H speaks again from the Flame of White.

"Pensatia," and his voice sounded with all the keys of heaven and earth, "all disciples start at the base of the Flame and work up to its exalted summit. In this heavy whiteness of Mist of the Gods, the student stays until he can converse freely in the vibrational code of Isis. Step by step, as in his earthly lessons and discipline, so also begin his lessons and discipline in the inner school. As he obeys, learns and does, so will his ascent in the Flame be, until finally he and the Flame are wedded in eternal bliss and service.

"It is not easy for the student to stand on this new territory. It takes all the trust and faith of a true disciple of the Rose. For as in the outer, so also do the Masters test and try one in their early lessons in this inner school. Each

Master will put many appearances before the pupil. Almost it seems at times that all that has been told is a cruel mockery, a fantasy woven by the Devil himself. Now, if the student is well grounded, he knows without a doubt that these appearances are only tests, that in spite of all objective deceptions the words of the Master are infallible. All that is spoken in the Flame of White will be.

"Unless one has inner faith, one is apt to flounder. It is only this deep abiding faith in God and the Masters which carries one safely up and through the Flame of White to pure authoritative knowledge and power. No Master can give this essential attribute. It is the key all must create for themselves. This I do say: Bare-headed under the Fire of Isis, if one believes with faith and obeys in the inner circle, no matter if all seems lost, if all weakness of the past appears to sweep down upon one, if you look up with shining eyes and heart to the garment of the Christus, up to the All-Seeing Eye, up to the love of the Blessed Mother, your tests will pass, and lo, the Master shall say to you, 'Well done, servant of the Rose.'

"So soldiers of the Flame, stand still at the base of Isis, drink of the red, the white and the blue. Stand still and get thy balance. Remember the hand of 'we the Masters' hold in safety all students who persevere. The base is the fiery furnace, the disciple's last testing ground. Pass this threshold, otherwise you are belched back into the outer. By the right of endeavor your efforts alone have brought you to the first round of the inner court. Only by your efforts can you stay.

"It is an idle wish to assume that in entering the base henceforth your rating is assured. Alas! That it were true. Sad, but drastically so, many go back. The Flame of Isis is too great a challenge, a sacrifice. They long for the familiarity of lesser vibrations.

"Faith was too weak to continue in the spiral of consciousness of immortality. They look back and close the door. Yet because of their journey thus far, God is kind. Mercy and compassion will bless their departure. Yet, the luster, the Jewel of the Lotus, is hidden. The mundane curtain of darkness shrouds the departed evermore in this incarnation from entering the inner school.

"Of his own free will, thusly did the student choose. For as one chooses for the high so shall one's strength be. God and the Masters never fail us. We fail ourselves.

"In our agony we have only to cry, 'Master, Master,' and pray to God the Father. Always we are heard, strength is given."

chapter ☆☆ THREE

"Up, up in the misty whiteness of the Flame of White, step by step climbs the dauntless disciple. Every step mastered carries the student to new awareness of cosmic dimensions. It is only in quietness of mind, heart and body that ascension in the Inner Flame is possible. The higher one goes in consciousness the clearer the infinite becomes. All our inner senses respond. We hear, see and feel from our interiors. With loving care the Master reveals to the zealous student lesson after lesson of cosmic signature. Every degree of its technique is given the pupil until he is able to carry back in positive activity the wisdom of the fourth dimension and above.

"As one obeys he progresses into all the planes. A panorama of 'flood gates' open at will and the disciple now gazes in infinite strata. Departed loved ones, great souls who have passed transitions' initiation are now accessible. The barriers of earth vibrations are lifted. The student in positive freedom now lives in heaven even as he lives on earth. In entering the White Flame he has finished with the astral and enters into the spiritual. The Holy of Holies, the Chalice of the Grail, henceforth is his. Therein one may sip and quaff the nectar of the Gods.

"Travelers of the Way of Rose and Lotus, think not that this is an idle promise. Today as you read there are beloved disciples reaping this conscious immortality in the Flame of White. They have stepped within, passed their initiation by fire. Now indeed they sit at the feet of their Master.

" 'When the student is ready the Master will appear.' *Here* is where this saying becomes a reality. Remember, no matter how dimly one perceives in this esoteric Flame, all is inevitable and true. Only the reality is realized here. Often the Hierarchy cast appearances that seem to counteract the mandates of the Absolute. Remember this is only to test the pupil's integrity of will and purpose. So as a little child, let go of your mortal gage and with uplifted joy, walk through the clouds of earth deception. The Christus shall lay within your hands all that is ordained for you.

"The technique of the Flame of White interferes in no way with mundane affairs. No seclusion, in common parlance, is needed. The disciple now, anytime, anywhere with open eyes, may enter the cosmic dimension. This profound door of illumination opens by the touch of the golden key built by the long discipline of the Way. Now the Christus, Masters, the God of all peoples welcome and give him the Kingdom."

The words of this third chapter are sealed by the hand of Master H himself. The All-Seeing Eye bears witness to the Pen of the Word.

I Pensatia, only the amanuensis of the vigil, pray for strength to ever ascend into the whiteness of the Flame. And may strength be given all who read to choose aright.

"Love is the essence of the Flame of White. Until it is experienced on the Path, one is not ready for the climactic cleavage and entrance.

"Nothing save Love, forgiving, compassionate, Christ-like can prepare the way to Isis' Light. Let us seek therefore to eliminate hate, envy, jealousy, competition, ambition, self-ego-power and turn our heart to Rose and Cross, bear and transmute *all* in Love. Else all travel esoterically is of no avail. Love only can lift karma and bear one up and beyond the cross to God and the Masters. All attributes are nothing without this cosmic vibration. It must become a living part of the pupil before he dares ever knock at the inner gate.

"Love is the final touch to the Key to the Light of Egypt. It must color the aura of every student of the White Brethren. Through pain, sorrow, loss, darkness and crucifixion, Love is fertilized and brought to bloom. At its awaking the heart opens. Then the student is truly on the way to Love's altar in the Flame of White and the supreme initiation.

"No one but God and the Masters know when love has reached the point of cleavage into the Lotus. Remember this, disciples-to-be. When you make obeisance to this Light, when the great initiation takes place, and you pass the angels three, you will know without a doubt that Love alone brought you there.

"As you climb the Stair of Flame, love will guide you. In fact you are love and love is you. So will love of one and many be granted all who attain this mandate.

"That which is no longer ours shall pass from us, that which bears our inner signature shall come quickly to the waiting, worthy heart. All who abide in the Flame of White shall reap perfect self expression and their divine destiny.

"So be faithful, dare to stand still and obey the Inner Flame. So will Heaven serve you in fullness and power. All the wonders celestial will be bequeathed to you. All will be clothed with the Cloth of Gold, the Magi's Robe, the Wand of Moses. The Staff of Light, Life and Love will be given all to use for humanity."

chapter ☆☆ **FIVE**

Again spoke Master H from the Flame of White:

"I will now discuss seeing in the spiritual focus of the Gods. Very few, if any, see distinctly when first entering the Hall of White. Sense and feeling—a certain inner awareness supercedes sight for the time being. The student must first get his walking legs steady before the 'sights' of the Gods are open for him.

"Here as in the outer school the student must work, and do spiritual exercises given him by the Master for the use of his inner eye. For though the cleavage has taken place he is as it were a new born babe in an ethereal plane of reality. Therefore, time must be spent learning to adapt the esoteric eye, that it may pierce the brightness and behold the unending pictures of the Word.

"Slowly, as the disciple obeys and uses his eye of Shiva, daily he learns to see as clearly in the White Flame as in earth vibrations. Little by little the Master, according to the disciple's inner strength, takes him higher into the realm of the inner circle, and aids him to penetrate through the brilliant mist of ever circling white.

"As one learns to 'see', so must he be able to discriminate and learn all the signatures of heavenly objects. Here as in the outer school love only gives power to behold, know and find. The prayer of the heart is mighty and toil-some here. It stirs the Word to active giving to the student.

"All pure desires find realization under the gaze of Isis. At first faintly, like a gossamer etching, objects, people, scenery and writing comes before the inner eye. But if patient, obedient and studious to that so delicately per-ceived, soon the disciple will notice progress. Keener and more graphic will become his sight. There will come the hour when all the glory of cosmic vision will be his. 'The Voice of the Silence' will be as readable as the earth pages. Thy Master will reveal himself in the clear virile presence of his immortality. Thy cleavage has taken place, all thy centers are quivering, as a race horse well trained ready to start for the final race of attainment. Thy God and Master who hold the reins will surely ride you to victory. Like a horse who pulls for his master, so pupil, ride the white horse through the Flame of White to Shangri-la and the flower of the 9th vibration.

"Yet do not try to see too rapidly in the higher dimen-sion. Let the White Chalice of the Grail give of its light to thee. As a child, be spontaneous, full of faith and ex-pectancy. Believe all the Master reveals, no matter how faint. For if you do not believe when the sight is dim, if you do not embrace what is shown you, then vision will not expand and clear sight is denied you. So study what is given you and in some manner take its value back to earth and give out to all who come across thy path.

"Now in closing the 5th chapter let it be known that the gentle love of the Christus forms the circle of protec-tion to all who enter herein. He is the Good Shepherd, you are His flock. The Rose and the Flame, the inner school, is the inner wire which connects one with cosmic consciousness. 'Knock and it shall be opened unto you' . . . 'Ask what you will, it will be.' So speaks the Master of Masters. So echo all the Masters in White."

"Come, Pensatia," spoke Master H out of the Flame of White. "Let me show you the waters of life flowing eternally—Be not afraid, just follow me," he directed.

With awe and wonder I obeyed. . . . Higher and higher we climbed in consciousness, getting closer to the center of whiteness. The Master seemed to propel me upward and forward. I realized that it was only through his aid that I traveled in so high a vibration.

On either side beautiful scenery of mountains, meadows and valleys were visible, changing with rapidity. Friendly, happy people were at ease. Colorful birds flew from bright green trees. Animals of many species ran and played through the countryside.

Higher we climbed, or ascended. Now and then I caught a glimpse of people I had known on earth . . . We ascended still higher, always in spiral form . . . Suddenly a host of angels bore down upon us. Each played a musical instrument which blended into an immortal symphony. Then it was Master H pulled me back and bade me be still and look.

A rush of silver waters came coursing through the center of White Flame. Power, vivifying, purifying and electrified swirled in mighty current through and around it until it was lost in a dazzle of golden light brighter than the sun.

I looked. Master H bent forward and did speak a word in the name of love, and behold! the waters were calm as a still mirror and wide as a margin of flat ribbon. He cupped his hands, did drink and bade me do likewise. He spoke: "He who sees and stands still and drinks of this shall have everlasting life, have access to all knowledge and power. All students who enter the inner school and stay, shall, must and will drink of the waters of life.

"By the use of the law of love they still the currents and can drink and bathe in its stream at will in safety. By the law of attraction love obeys love, and love, the vivifying essence of the waters, obeys always the call of love. Here in the waters of life, when prepared, the disciples bathe, drink and look into the cosmic waters for the reflection of the mandates from heaven which are pictured therein. Here, to all in a different way, Baptism takes place: the coming of the Holy Ghost, the Alchemical Marriage, the descent of the Doves of Heaven. When this transpires the student becomes a true disciple of the Master.

"Until these initiations are realized by the student, God and the Masters know, he cannot be trusted fully to carry out his earthly mission. Harken now to this infallible mandate embedded forever in the Fire of Isis: 'All students who embrace the waters of life, they who are Baptized in its current, they who meet the 'Bridegroom' shall have the power and authority to start, do and carry out their mission in life.' They will be told and given their orders. The Masters know they will obey to the nth degree. No matter how hard the task, or long, humble, strange or famous, the disciple will carry through and be silent.

"So students of the inner circle, when thou comest from thy Holy Baptism, rest in the Lord, let go and await word from the Master. Within the time of three, new orders will come.

"Let thy experience meanwhile mellow into serene exultation. Let thy prayers be in the heart, that sacred entrance to the corridor of the illumined. Live naturally, enter the table of the Christus, and in some three, your orders will come."

"Write today, Pensatia, of the Sun of the Absolute," dictated Master H from the banks of the Waters of Life.

"Look," he said, pointing upward at that circle of golden light of which the physical sun is a reflection. "Here in the inner school the disciples strengthen and utilize their awakened interiors, until step by step they climb the circular stairway of the Rose leading to the citadel of pure Gold of the Hidden One. As they obey and carry out their orders they ascend into the Flame of White. Thus one is able to approach the golden disc, the splendor of the God of Gods.

"No disciple or mortal master ever drank from the heart of the Gold. Up, up to the golden rays they can and do reach the esoteric tower, lit by the Sun of the Absolute for the beloved disciples and Masters alone.

"Here all who are ready gather at the sound of the cosmic gong and bathe in the gold even as they have bathed in the white, the silver blue and the red. This is the highest round, the ultimate of mortal endeavor, while living in earthly body. No one may go beyond the golden light into the Gold Itself. This is the privilege, the grace of those of and beyond the Third Degree of Christ and the Buddha, the Degree of Perfection, of absorption into the golden heart of the Creator.

"The Third Degree is the nearest one may attain in mortal body. Very rarely and of his own choice does a disciple choose to go beyond the Third. For if so all human ties must be severed. Alone one must ascend to the Disc of Ra.

"The preceding Degree is as important as the Third and beyond. Either way the disciple chooses is to the glory of God and the Masters. Often, karma and one's mission call for the human ties of marriage and children. If in the past incarnation a marriage has not been experienced in its innate beauty, then one must master and transmute such into its esoteric fulfillment, else one can not and dare not choose a higher altitude of service. Only under the law of cause and effect can the disciple choose.

"Obedience to spiritual law and to the Master's orders is imperative. When disciples have passed in victory the lesser degrees of the inner circle, then, and only then are they eligible to aspire to the greater role, that of ascension into the Gold of the Absolute. After once choosing, only as Christ Rays or in Bodies of Light do they migrate to earth vibrations. Never do they assume earth bodies again. Lesser Masters have that power. But the super signature of the Absolute has no earthly mandates, no earthly wires. Henceforth they who choose and are accepted are absorbed, or Masters of the Hierarchy of the Cosmic Host. All other masters, adepts, disciples may reach up in purity of heart and catch the words of wisdom which ever beam in spiral radiation from the Gold through the Flame of White.

"It is from this reservoir of the Cosmic Hierarchy that the laws of the Cosmos flow forth, and the mirror of Akasha was formed. Here the creative Waters of Life gush from the heart of the King of Kings. With scepter of dazzling love, in justice and power does the Eye of Shiva look down and see all. From the Creator's beat goes forth the gong for all acts of earth. Birth, marriage, death, all major climaxes, changes, opportunities, open and closed doors, happen only when the gong of Heaven sounds. Down, down through the spiral of white does the strike of the gong sound and echo to earth. Only to disciples is it a conscious occasion. To those not Cosmically aware, they speak of fate or luck. Yet the disciple knows all is self-made cause and effect, and by love's initiation only does the gong ring out from the Disc of Golden Flame. They know at each sound, the Infinite is speaking, saying: 'It shall be.'

"Sometimes the disciple's inner hearing is not yet keen enough. Then the Master relays the message, or fiat of the Word, and why it sounds. Remember this, always when the gong sounds, the time has arrived for certain things to come to pass in one's earthly life. At that moment, from the first strike of the gong, that which is conceived 'within' slips into objective birth. When a Master tells you the gong has sounded, and this or that will be, know, and with steadfast faith wait and behold the 'fruit of the Path.' Even as Solomon stated, 'There is a time for everything.' In the Flame of White each student realizes the infinite truth of this saying. For the Wheel of Birth, of action and reaction, is revealed.

"One knows the mathematical certainty of spiritual law. Everything is by law and order. Supreme justice prevails. When certain vibrational keys are struck all comes to pass. Vibrating to that note nothing may be forced—if so it crumbles. Only what is earned and written 'self-made' in the Scroll of Gold comes forth.

"When the Word went out the divine destiny of all mankind also became law. In minute degree every act and thought that has been and will be is etched in God's sacred heart. The whole only God knows and They absorbed in Gold. The lesser Masters, (only lesser because they are not fully absorbed in the Absolute), they, as God permits, are shown the destiny of every pupil. All their work with the disciples is to hasten the sounding of the gong.

"If it were not for the age-old Path of the Masters, countless ages would pass before humanity made any progress. . . . Rejoice esoteric disciples. Every prick and pain, every nail of negative karma transmuted, makes nearer the hour when the Cosmic Gong shall strike. Thus bringing to pass all the Masters' words and that which is written divinely for each man and woman. This is not blind fate, but the divine design coming forth—beautiful, uplifting, free, containing only love and joy.

"Everyone has freedom to choose, to go with their divine scroll, or away from it. As we decide we make our own fate. Either it is in harmony with God's mandate, or else we create negative pictures into Akasha. Then only by tears, loss, tragedy, their divine mission and heritage is darkened. Through self-made karma one has to unweave the wrong threads we ourselves have sown into the bloom of life."

chapter ☆☆ **EIGHT**

Up through the Flame of White to the Waters of Life; on through its majestic sweep, Master H guided me to the lofty summit of the mount of illumination. "Come," he said, "seat yourself on this snowy whiteness of altitude. Write as I picture the essence of all wisdom.

"Here is the mount of Cosmic Consciousness. Here, all disciples must abide before the star of authority is blazed in indelible fire upon their foreheads. Its cool, clear atmosphere must be breathed and absorbed. Its foursquare scenic splendor all students esoteric must perceive and understand. The true vision of divinity is revealed on the mountain top of the Illuminati. Here the ultimate of the Absolute is thundered in mighty notes to the disciple. In naked white light with bared head the disciple looks up as he stands upon the awe inspiring mountain top of illumination. God seems to step down. His words sound forth on the holy mountain infallible mandates from the Cosmic Hierarchy.

"Alone, except for the Master, the disciple walks and studies in the brilliant letters of his orders. He rests and partakes of the manna of the Masters. At last 'Home' is found in the abode of the White Brethren. Shangri-la is open house to the disciple's feet. He is a privileged comer and goer of every part and parcel of that august place.

"Until one is able to ascend this mountain the Master never reveals himself in complete regalia. On this citadel Cosmic Initiation for every disciple takes place at the appointed moment. Power is given the ready disciple. He has blazed through the crucibles and transmuted base elements in the Flame. Now the great initiation in the 'Air' of the afflatus of the zenith of illumination is his.

"Not until all lesser initiations take place can this climax happen. To reach the lofty altar of Isis one must have left behind all earth vibrations. The Path will see to that. Until one has and gives up, until one has not and receives, until joy and sorrow both have embraced one, the student is not ready, and never can be. Rest assured, before the veil of the mount is lifted, and you are called to climb its high spiral to the supreme initiation of all, you will have supped of ecstasy and drank of earth sorrow. You will have known the gold of earth and are ready for the gold of heaven.

"Let us assume," continued Master H, "by right of conquest the student has arrived at this momentous mount of awareness, where he lives in the aura of the Hierarchal Host. Here the grueling vibrations of earth do not exist. The rare companionship of Master and disciple is a conscious reality here. The inner commands now and changes all outer weakness into strength and beauty. On this sacred esoteric mountain the disciple is capable in ever greater degrees of holding the Light of Isis. The purified air pours upon him until his inner and outer pair and become impregnated with its potent flame.

"It is a grace and privilege, this sojourn on the mount of illumination. There in the snows of its summit the Master prepares the disciple for the dynamic birth of all his powers, interior and exterior. If the initiation here is finished—one becomes a magi, ripe for lesser mastership, or greater. On this mountain top all rituals and outer lessons are eliminated. First-hand the disciple receives and studies from the Master and the cosmic archives. No barriers exist. The Master hears and answers the pupil and instructs.

"It is this tutelage on the mountain top which is the flowering of all the preceding steps on the Wisdom Path. It is the crowning diploma of all the student's efforts on the Way of the Rose. In the white bracing air of the White Brethren and the immortal beams from the Eye of the Hidden One, each disciple sits at the feet of his beloved Master, learns, obeys and grows into his holy initiation sublime.

"Often, a long time, perhaps several incarnations must pass before here on the summit the Royal Signature of the Illuminati is earned. Yet it is possible, and there are students, and will be again, those who receive the 'Mark of Isis' in this incarnation. How long it takes depends on the zeal, obedience and unselfish love of each disciple. Is the pupil willing to pledge still a part of every day to the tasks given by the Master? . . . Remember, now the tempter seeks to divorce the aspirant from his culminating victory. A duplicate of the Dark Night overwhelms the heart and endeavors to persuade the disciple that the mount of illumination is not for him.

"Know O seekers of the Keys of Life, if faithful to God and the Masters, the duality of all temptations will not avail. Here in the eternal snows of the flute of Ra your victory is assured. The Masters infallible hold in escrow the secret jewel of attainment. They lay with their hands the esoteric brand upon the forehead of every initiate who has come through the Holy Trial and Air of the Mount.

"Many false orders come at this stage of soul evolution. Almost one will believe it is the Master's will to do thus and thus. Yet remember, in prayer and meditation one will know the real. At this time some may feel they are doing nothing for humanity. Yet such is not true. O disciples, obey the inner mandates in the heart. There only will the Master speak true. Obey all that is given at the beginning, as no new orders will be until you have fulfilled the old.

"Here in the inner school law and order prevails. Obedience must precede all other objectives. Know also if a Master decrees a thing it will be. So at this epochal cycle on the Rosy Path forbear thy earthly work. Know now is the crucial period when your cosmic destiny is at hand. Just as you are able to stand in the Flame of White, the Christus and the Masters are preparing each and every one.

"Faint not when all the Master says seems not to come at the appointed moment. Remember, until the disciple's faith is without a doubt, and unshakable, nothing will objectify. So in the darkness of the Path, at all stages and times keep your faith burning as a lamp of heaven. Let no finite conception or deception mar thy faith in thy Master's words spoken from the inner circle in the swirling Flame of White.

"Know always the Master's love surrounds you. Ask now what you will—it shall be granted you, be it of earth or heaven. Do not hesitate to voice thy desires, even though they are already known. Yet it is the law, one must ask. Remember Christ's words: 'Seek first the Kingdom of Heaven and all else will be given you.' "

chapter ☆☆ NINE

"Write, Pensatia, of the Golden Flame," spoke Master H standing in the whiteness of the Mountain Top.

"As the disciple sojourns here, at the appointed time he is told to bathe in the Flame of Gold that showers from the Absolute Itself. Not until the student has attained the basic technique and absorbed the white light is it possible to walk under and drink of the golden strength of this essence of regeneration, the overflow of the Creator's Love. To be worthy to bathe in its dazzling rays is to know one's self-conscious state of divinity.

"Daily contact with the Gold burns the final signature of Isis on the heart of every disciple. Herein is the secret of the Rosy Cross revealed. This happens when in dedication we lay ourselves upon the altar for God's use and service.

"The first step into the Gold acquaints one with the stir of God speaking direct to soul of man. It is the true court of justice, law and mercy. Here under the majesty of its rays the disciple enters his final crucible, only this time it is a crucible of the fourth dimension, a crucible of the glory of God pouring down upon those disciples who work, pray and obey in the Golden Flame. It is the crucible which brings expression to the now awakened centers. To be allowed to bathe in its splendor spells health and vitality.

"No Master bids a disciple enter this Flame of Gold unless regeneration is decreed for the physical body. When one enters the 'Golden Shower' one's passports are assured. Health of mind and body is and will be no matter how deceptive outer symptoms and appearances. You are *whole* in the Flame. Remember, you need naught but divine meditation now. Accept that and know all else will be added as needed. No Master would dare open the spiral of Gold unless one was ready. This bath accentuates and increases one's earthly life. It makes visible the Master and brings speech and creative power to all thy interiors. The love and fruitage of the soul comes forth. Pray within its eternal wisdom and great and swift will be thy answers, disciples of the Rose.

"This Flame of Gold is the loving breath of the Good

Shepherd, the Father's benediction. It is the glory after the travail. To walk in its love rays will transmute the lesser into the higher, all weakness into strength, ugliness into divine beauty. Here the prodigal returns to the 'Fatted Calf', all that the Father has is his for the asking. Celestial music breaks forth for his inner ears, the flute of Ra plays the notes of Mastery. The All-Seeing Eye looks down through the Golden Flame and says: 'Fear not, my beloved disciple, you have sought the Kingdom of Heaven first, all else shall be added. Be happy and of good cheer. Walk, obey the Master's voice and great and long will be thy life and service on earth for thy brothers of all races.'

"This is the last purifying Flame, which separates all dross, and leaves one born in the essence of Gold. So continue to stay in its eternal vibrations, and fear not if at the beginning the stay is trying. Only know, if told to enter, you will triumph with victory regardless of all appearance of sickness. For often the student feels symptoms of illness—yet he will not succumb. It is only the Gold working out the dross.

"Call 'Master, Master' . . . yet stay bravely in the Golden Flame. Nothing of harm can happen—neither mind or body will be ill. For as said before: No one enters the Flame of Gold until ready to stand its potent power. So make oneself at home, in long or short intervals it matters not, for God and the Masters watch thy every move. They will not fail you. By your obedient effort you have entered. You will be sustained. Your illumination is promised.

"Have you asked for anything? Know already it is yours. Give thanks, for in the Flame of Gold, like a miracle when you least expect, all desires of the heart are granted the worthy disciple."

"High up in the center of this Gold," continued the Master H, "is the Altar of Altars where, in prostrate supplication, the disciple prays for the grace of the Most High to flood his consciousness with Light, Life and Love, to use for the evolvement of darkness and ignorance.

"All disciples who kneel in consciousness, or stand at the Altar of the Inner Rose of the Golden Dawn, shall receive the grace of the Word and go forth equipped with the power to do. Remember God is a God of Love, Compassion. The Good Shepherd will bless and give you Love; all life will sense the aura of your soul powers.

"Here the disciple takes his vows. Thy Master shall instruct you, until in full you sip freely of the Holy Grail. Cast out all fear, say in a loud voice: 'In the name of Love, begone all negative shadows, all false appearances. Let clarity and strength of mind and body be mine. So mote it be.' Bow thy heart upon the life of the Rose, and ask that you arise a new person, reborn in the White and the Golden Flame of the Christus. Let your blood flow warm with the Love of the Rose flowing through you and out to all life.

"Yes, disciples, let this spirit be thy prayer as you await your greatest initiation. To each in a different way will come the glorious blossom of the Path. Obey what is told. Always let three days and nights be spent in supplication, foregoing all earthly pleasures. (Meaning), remain at thy altar even in the midst of all thy objective activities. If faithful your Star will be given you. Arising from your vigil, you will come forth an Adept of the Path.

"All your innate desires must first be laid at the altar of the Rose and Lotus if you would reap the 'well done' of the Christus. Then in Akasha will one enter the Table of our Lord. There flashing from the Christus' hand will be the 'Cup of the Grail.' Even so, Blessed Mary, purity su-

105

preme, will call out: 'Behold my Son. He is the Way, the Truth, the Life of all mankind. In, through and by him ever live the illuminated of the Rose. Saints, Angels, the Hierarchy have their conclave here at the Inner Table. Come, mankind, enter the mystery school within. Brave the crucible of Gold. Know first-hand my heart of Love beating for all humanity, understanding your woes. Reach unto me, Mother of the Christ Babe. As you do, even so you reach to God, the Son and Holy Ghost. Ever do I intercede for you.'

"Even as we heed her words, joy will ride the morning winds. At the zenith of some noon hour one's heart will leap into its esoteric harvest. As you receive give back. All nature will serve you who are a greater servant. Heed all that is given in the Golden Flame, for potent is the message depicted from the Eternal Flow.

"At the Immaculate Table where ever sits the Christ, come in reverence, bow down and listen. Hear Him say to each disciple: 'Thou art whole, go forth in peace. In thy heart sing like a bird of the morning skies. Fight not, but live in brotherhood straight, eternally young with the nectar of the Absolute for thy nourishment as well as nature's abundance. With gracious deeds and thoughts cover thy walking mission. Laugh much and hurry not to gain temporal things. Rather ever hunger for the divine in all life.' "

Now I did with Master H ascend in consciousness in Cosmic Light. Master H pointed out a mighty Book suspended in triangular form. The All-Seeing Eye from the apex gazed down upon it.

"Behold, Pensatia, the Book of Love. From center of the Godhead flows this Book down to earth for all mankind to read when able. The pure love signature shines like a golden jewel for all humanity. Here are the written records of all true mating sealed by the Pentagram proclaiming the Alchemical Marriage. Only through the Flame of

White does the disciple have the power to read therein. From this infinite scroll all immortal books are inspired and brought forth on earth. Love alone is the great instigator of everything. . . . Look," directed Master H.

Turning, the pure gold for a split second almost blinded my vision. Then, in a cool blue spray of dew mist, my soul consciousness lifted to a white and Holy gate. All fell from me save my cape of white, which I wrapped about my naked self.

Gone was Master H. I stood alone on the citadel of the Book of Love in the Flame of White. Fragrant rose petals fluttered through the cosmic air. The Book flew open. "Read, Pensatia," echoed in the distance the beloved voice of the Master.

At first all seemed but symbols, which as I pondered upon became written words. (Afterwards the Master told me, by symbols first then by words, does the objective mind pick up cosmic truth). The inner signature of man, bird and beast and all nature was etched indelibly here. I desired to see my page and there it was, past, present and future. Some pages were closed, no symbols or word could I read. Only that which the disciple can face is permitted. What was revealed I kept in my heart, so I could ponder and study upon that received.

I discovered that if there was a rapport between one and others, it was possible to read from this Cosmic Book for others when they were unable to do so. Conscious clairvoyance became a fact here. The reality back of its three dimensions became plain. Only in conscious awareness does one feel the Love Rays pouring through the Flame of White for man and earth. Only in conscious oneness with the Father may we utilize our divinity. From this Cosmic Record, our cause and effect of life after life shows the eternity of the Now.

As our inner centers open we revolve with our divine signature. Thus only is Cosmic Illumination born for man.

Then our bodies obey and follow the inner Word. We are in reality living flames of light, life and love. All that is written in this fiat will be objectified. Here from this Book of Flame all gongs are sounded for the great transition. One keeps the body only as long as earth life is stamped on the infinite ledger. We can not change our hour of departure. Only the grace of God may impregnate past karma and grant a stay on earth. We ask and await the Father's will.

The exodus across the River Styx is the true democracy. All must meet as One here, King and commoner alike. Only the awakened and illuminated may by grace, if it be the Father's will, go beyond his alloted time. To live long on earth one must have in his blood and bone the divine mixture of the Elixir and Stone. The fabled Powder must impregnate the physical body in Christed resurrection. It must be liberated Light, thus regenerating the body in active acquiessence of immortality. The Golden Ray from the Flame of White must, from top to toe, be consciously experienced. When we ourselves become Love, then all that the Father has is ours. Love is the open sesame of the Holy Ghost.

chapter ☆☆ ELEVEN

Again I keep my vigil. Master H leads with candle flame my steps into the White. Within my heart is warmth, and love fire embraces my consciousness. I sit in esoteric fashion there in the White of Heaven's hearth.

"Pensatia," spoke the Master, "gaze now in the mirror of the heart and pen as you receive."

I did scan the cosmic lines upon the heart's scroll. I saw

a mighty train come streaming into port. People, one by one debarked, and in white robes came and sat with me upon the cosmic greenway. Always words formed beneath the symbol.

"People when ready rise in consciousness to Love dimension and settle on the cosmic hearth and receive ever as you. By meditation they absorb wisdom."

Now a second symbol revealed itself. A "7" in red fire was silhouetted in the spiral of Akasha. I felt a great and holy stillness impregnated in this "7." Again the print of Akasha rolled before my inner eye.

"All must become the sacred '7' before the heart reveals in full for them. All must partake of its inner quiet. Its spirituality must sing for all its calm, eternal music within blood, bone and soul, before the OM of God lifts the Veil of Isis.

"Not until '7' purifies and synthesizes all duality of Maya will the disciple realize the heart is his eternal home. It takes 7 years, 7 steps, 7 initiations, aye, 7 lives, unless by grace of God, to lift the mundane weight of illusion into the realm of the sacred '7'. When the pupil has so ordered his life and obeyed the discipline and lived from the heart's call he will surely gain the signature of '7'.

"No intellectual reading of esoteric books can inject the cosmic fluid of the 7th *sound, color, word* and *action* upon the disciple. One must by Soul Alchemy alone deserve and bring the peace and glory of the '7' within his consciousness.

"Remember after attaining the '7', one is quiet, dignified and fortified with the ultra spiritual key of this mystic '7'. Its power transforms and makes luminous all lesser things. It is the cosmic mother of numbers bringing softness and clear intuition to one.

"The inverted, unawakened negative side of 7 is depleting, weak and shilly-shally. Those with a 7 birth path must find the inner realm of 7, or they are lost in Maya's illusion. The mandate infallible of '7' is: Find the inner initiation of my number.''

Now a silver star five-pointed formed against the cosmic screen of Love in the Flame of White. It undulated in vibrational quickness, like mercury.

"Silver is the quintessence of mutability. None attain the Red Powder of the Gods, or the Alchemical Gold, until the five pointed star of silver pours through one's fivefold expression.'' So interpreted the symbolic star to my heart's consciousness.

"Silver is the cooling fusion of love's all. Without its balancing effect love's ardor would be chaotic. The signature of the silver star is ingrained upon all initiations on the mountain top. It calms and lowers the electrical power and cosmic fire of love into objective expression.

"Even those who wear only outward silver are more stable than those who wear gold only. In all esoteric and exoteric expression silver is imperative for balance. Before Cosmic Illumination is attained the silver waters of Baptism must flow through one's interiors. All disciples must partake of the silver drink. The silver star must be ingrained upon the rose center of the heart. By Holy Mary and the Christus, silver heals and tempers, bringing firmness to all it touches. It is the middle denominator of the Way, soothing the paradoxes of the Way and liquidating the froth and nonessentials of the climb to the Holy Grail.

"Christ attained the blessing of silver in Jordan stream. Henceforth the essence of the five pointed star was His to Crucifixion, Resurrection, and Ascendency in Isis. It was the potent, adhesive power of the silver star of God that gave Him strength to carry through and suffer. Always God the Father gives to every disciple the cosmic and mundane balance of silver.

"All gold has a base of inner silver to create equality of essence. Ponder on this. Remember, all insanity, karmic or otherwise, is caused by a lack of silver. The fires of love must be tempered in the cool, steadfast waters of quick-silver, which, though ever running, is a benediction of fusion quality. As the disciple immerses in its silver flow, slowly but surely there comes a holy moment in the heart's altar when the silver synthesizing of the Way, emerges into the wholeness of the five pointed star. Then, and then only, does one know: the outer and inner are One."

chapter ☆☆ TWELVE

My blessed Master came. Through the dusk of night came he close, and spoke:

" 'The Flame of White' is finished. Faithfully thou hast traveled and penned the truth as I revealed. Readers, ponder well. Other books shall be scribed by you, Pensatia: three times three, ere the New Age blossoms. All shall be published. And one you knew in long past lives you shall meet, and lo, he will bring to public view each and every manuscript. And the way will open, in all ways materially and otherwise, to publish them. So have I spoken. And even so, Pensatia, ever shall you be cared for; even so shall all spoken for you come forth. Even so he who sees that my works are published, I shall bless greatly cosmically and otherwise.

"Now I go. Several years hence I give you your first book to be published.* There will be times when it seems impossible the fulfillment of thy mission. Yet with faith and obedience, Pensatia, carry on through the dark hours even though ridiculed and crucified and all tangible assets

*"A Journey Into the Light" privately printed, New York, 1958.

dissolve. Daybreak shall come and the way shine like the sun upon the works I send forth.

"This finale, the 12th chapter, is short. Blessed is thy pen, and blessed those who aid in the publication, and more blessed is the message within to every reader who ponders and heeds.

"Arise and enter the Path leading to the Flame of White. Thus will the Holy Grail be yours, and the influx of the Christed Man come forth. Even so shall my blessing ever be with you. Remember 'when the student is ready the Master appears.' Let this be *you* and *you* and *you*, beloved readers.

"Now I salute each and everyone with compassion and love and a deep understanding of all your past and present karma. Fear not to face the new frontiers of the New Age. With the tools of the alchemical secret of the Rose of Life, and the example of the lowly Lotus, arise and give birth to the Divine Cosmic Heritage which belongs to all Humanity.

"Now I, Master H, depart for the Highlands of the Soul, the High Mountain of which Pensatia shall write in the time of ripeness. This book has been in Akasha, in the alpha and omega of the Word, though only now does it objectify in print. Peace Profound to the whole wide world, to nature, and my beloved people."

·   ·   ·
·   ·
·

THE ROSE OF LIFE

PRELUDE

Into my earth pilgrimage walks the Master H.

As quietness steals upon me, in shade of tree, hotel lobby, or by cool of river, comes he, beloved Guru of my soul.

"Write," he speaks, in positive gentle tone. "Write of The Rose of Life. *Descend with me into the cave of darkness and rise to witness thy birth of* The Rose of the Golden Dawn.*"*

He placed his hand upon my head, saying, "Blessings be yours, and unto all who find the Way and obey."

Music, simple, profound, resounded from my soul down through my heart and out to earth so green.

As quietly as he came, so went Master H.

Yet, with my pen will I follow and record this travelogue.

PENSATIA

Dedicated to Claire
in friendship and for a service
gratefully remembered.

chapter ✩ ONE

Again, the Master came, saying, "The Rose of Life, would you know, Pensatia? Then follow me."

I arose and did his bidding . . . We started on a Path winding upward, over and through earth. I left all behind, bade farewell to all familiar landmarks. In simple attire, even as he came, I obeyed.

Darkness was, and my heart was sad, for home and earth looked bright, and all joys seemed behind, and the Rose so far away. Yet the Master's call, and the inner voice, was greater, more compelling than any earthly gain.

"Grieve not, Pensatia," spoke the Master, "you will return. They who seek the Rose, only travel that they may return with Holy Gifts and Sacred Graces. Now, keep heart and eyes upon the Path. One goal, one purpose: to attain the luminous petals of the White Eternal Rose."

Even as he spoke my heart grew lighter. Strength and a sweet peace stirred within me. I minded not the darkness, or that the winds bore harsh upon us—even when pain rent body and feet, following the Master through dimness and strange lands.

"Be not dismayed, Pensatia. The Path lies through all experiences: past, present and future. One only seems to have lost the familiar, while learning to see from the inner dimensions of cosmic reality instead of only objectively.

"When at the upward pinnacle of our journey, holding full bloom the Rose, then will all which bears one's signature be returned. There, in cosmic vantage point, one will know the glory, the victory of the Golden Dawn, that lifting of the mundane veil into the clear vision of the fourth dimension and above."

As the Master conversed, we were progressing slowly and steadily upon the Path. Plant, human and animal life became most interesting, since the Light of the Master's aura penetrated into all darkness, which made possible the

115

communion with everything. Yet, in traveling, my body often felt weak, ill, and a great nausea fell upon me. Almost I cried out to turn back. Then it was that the Master did lay his hand upon my head, and bade me rest, and he did give me a green liquid, brewed from the earth's heart. Drinking, strength came to walk on.

"Always," explained the Guru, "the student who obeys and follows to seek the Rose, God and the Masters protect, heal, aid. When the going gets too rough, stop for a moment. Consciously let go, even of the Path. Then a sudden influx of Life will flood your being, and one is ready to take another step on the Path. Remember, obedience to leave all, to follow, to tread the Path, which is very dark at the onset, are one's credentials to the Rose of Roses. Dare all and you will receive all. For, at the summit, where the Path turns to golden hue, where the Holy Cross and the Rose blooms triumphant, white and most powerful, one will kiss and remember every step upon the Way as a precious birth into Light, Life and Love."

It was now pitch black, the road was rocky and my bare feet stumbled.

"Come, student," spoke the Master, "we bed for the night. Always must the Pilgrim of the Rose observe the Laws of Nature and God as they pertain to the physical body. Rest, sleep and food are requirements along the esoteric journey; as well as play, recreation, joy."

Even as he talked, the rough Path seemed a soft, soothing bed. Soft breezes, music, like unto a lullaby, sounded through green trees which suddenly lined the way. Dancing elves, beautiful forms of people walking to and fro, were seen. Our hearts and thoughts seemed to blend with them. Then, as I relaxed, I perceived home and loved ones. A closer bond was felt.

"You see," came soft the Master's voice, "how the Path, even at the beginning, brings a realization, a sprouting seed of peace and brotherhood. When the Rose thou hast attained, Pensatia, then will one be all things to all life—and life will be all to one. So, persevere, all who seek to know."

Oh, how blessed the sleep, if only for a moment, upon the Path of the Rose. All burdens seem lifted. One knows he has started the pilgrimage to the Holy Grail. Though weary, he rests with trust and faith that God and the Master are leading.

So it was. I awoke, and behold, the Path grew brighter. Lessons in slumber seemed to have been absorbed, as though through the evening hour, a cordelia had been handed me.

"Come," called the Master ahead, "we have a long way to go and much to learn."

It was a bright young morning and my spirit was high after the clean rest. Invigoration gave me stamina to obey. Taking hold of the Master's hand, we bore upward to the heights.

"Remember, Pensatia," spoke the Guru, "there comes many a time, before attainment, when I leave you on your own. Prepare for those moments, for, unless the disciple is integrated in the center within his own heart, the Path avails nothing but empty illusion and nonfulfillment. Yes, at certain periods on the Rosy Path, one must stand alone, even without the Guru's presence. So build strong and sure as we walk the Way together. Know, even when you see me not, in the shadows, I see, know, and ever watch the true student. When the student is ready, all Heaven, Nature, and the Hierarchy bring forth one's mission."

Listening to the Master, we often came to little hills and beautiful vistas. There we would sit and scan the earthly horizon. At such times he would point out the meaning of each stage of the ascent to the Rose. It was a most precious memory of the pilgrimage. Always gentle, yet firm of speech, understanding, compassionate, of mundane and cosmic virility and balance, he made clear the search.

"Pensatia, never hurry or rush. All wisdom is born of great stillness and patience. Even in one's earthly duties, karma and Caesar's tribute—easy like, gently fulfill thy cause and effect. Clearing, pushing through to the center of even measure, take earth and heaven, else the lack of balance throw one to the abyss.

"Always have time to pause and refresh thyself at these hill-marks and sylvan oases. These happy interludes, if only for moments, keep the student equal to climbing the summit within to the transcendent Rose of Life."

Indeed it was so. The rolling green hills, the woodland trees, the clear rivers, made the Path more easy to travel and gave the student stimulation and courage needed to progress.

"Always," intervened the Master, "let vision and imagination and heart warmth tune all thy efforts. For earth alone brings misery and stagnation.

"Come, let us up now, for, see yon cavern? There must we enter."

He turned, blessing me, making the sign of the cross, and, igniting the light within my heart, he bade me in God's name and Holy Christus, to enter, and be not afraid. Trusting in the Master, I found the Path descending into a cavern, most dark, chilly, empty of music, beauty, or life. Not even the Master was visible, though I felt the presence of his hand on mine. So dark it was I knew not where my foot would tread. Faith and trust only guided me through the long darkness. A whisper floated to my heart from the Guru.

"In this darkness, Pensatia, keep your consciousness on the heart, then will a subtle light lead you in safety through the many such milestones on the Path.

"Privileged indeed is the student who passes this cave in the discipline of the crucible and wins.

"Remember, seeking the Rose of Life is no idle jaunt.

It needs all the twelve ingredients of the Elixir. At each cycle of the Path a portion of the fabled Stone is built into the awareness of the disciple. So fear not, nor despair. At every obedient tread on the Path, one is closer to the immortality of the Rose. When all seems lost, and in vain, a mockery, only *obey*, *keep on*, ever look within to God, the Master, and Nature to guide one to Cosmic Consciousness, which *is* the Rose of Life. Always one experiences hours of blackness, rough and stormy weather, when it seems shipwreck is the answer. *Remember then thy heart's light* and love will surely see you over and beyond the stress of thy cause and effect.

"See," pointed Master H, "already the Path brightens, becomes smooth, lighted with a glowing Star. This blessed symbol is ever seen by the disciple after passing through darkness."

I did indeed behold a lustrous five pointed star. It warmed and did cheer my heart as though bidding all to follow the Wisdom Path. I felt victory to come, felt a promise of my divine destiny. A deep gratitude born of humility was in my soul, for I realized that only by grace and the Master's presence do we go thus far.

"By one's efforts, too," spoke he. "Always remember, one *earns* the Master's touch."

"Yes, Master, I know," I answered, "yet these obstacles none could meet without their beloved Guru, who has attained."

Now, I did thank the God of all people. Lilies sprang in lush growth upon the Path—a fragrance filled the air about us.

"Purity of zeal and heart-prayer-thanks are ever symbolized by lilies on the Path." He plucked one and laid its whiteness upon my heart, saying, "Ever, students of the Rose, keep pure thy motives, thy steps, deeds, that one be worthy to give birth to the immortal Rose.

"At the beginning of the climb to Azùl, or Isis unveiled, one often hesitates to follow all the way.

"When earthly objects, money, friends, love, all seem to depart; when death often takes away those close—here is the crucial test. When barren emptiness looms, when supply is cut off, many cease and go back into material gain. Yet the true disciple climbs on and up the Holy Ascension; on with humble adoration, faith and prayer, through the discipline, the crucibles, to the transcendent finale of all his efforts, the conscious awareness of the Rose of Life. Ponder well, Pensatia, for temptations to leave come to all. Even as one decides, so is karma liberated and soul destiny brought forth. At any dimension on the Path—yes, even when almost at the top—aye, the highest sometimes fail, and the neophyte comes up front because of childlike faith, and willingness to learn."

chapter ☆☆ TWO

Now, on my journey to the Rose, I drank often of bitter waters, often undergoing servile and menial work. Often my pockets were empty, my living quarters small and ugly. Yet, the goal was kept in sight, and agreement was made with my karma. Even as through loss, sorrow, change, storm—in pressing on, the Master came; that is, I felt his presence, his watching, silent, yet flowing to me subtle strength in my mundane labors.

And when the night hour arrived in my room close to the stars and heaven sky, the Star would light my heart, and the Path would brighten, opening up like a cathedral window for me to see in a higher dimension; until, month after month, there came a moment in the midst of meditation when the Master H led me into the sacred fire of the Heart, where, after a long stay in its crucible, I passed the first Holy Initiation upon the Path. Ever after a closer relationship grew between pupil and Guru.

Now, understanding and meaning became alive in the discipline. Meditating, talking with the Master, I learned, little by little, to carry back to earth the wisdom garnered.

I ponder now on one of the precious, rare talks the Master gave me in the Heart's Shekinah.

"Pensatia," so he spoke, "early on the Path students must learn to transmute the lesser into the higher, and the higher into the lesser until the two become one. Thus it is the hardships, trials, grief—all steps upon the Path must be Christed and flooded by degrees with the essence of the Rose. Only as one does this can they be known as disciples-to-be. Here within the Heart live the sacred wisdom teachings. To receive them, obedience and perseverance at all costs, is the way. Every duty, action, thought, must bear the stamp of the Master. They alone *know*, for they have trod the Way and know victory—illumination through self-mastery. To every neophyte walking the age-old Path, are tests, lessons, duties given, needed to build the Stone and the Elixir.

"No two students have quite the same experiences, though the end in view is always Cosmic Consciousness, or conscious at-one-ment with the Creator. Every student runs afoul the cause and effect self-generated. That which is weak and off-base from cosmic law must be transmuted or liquidated at each milestone upon the Path. Thus only can one progress. It is the Way to the Holy Grail, to the shining Star, to the Christ Babe in the manger.

"Now, Pensatia, see what happens as one steadily ascends the mountain."

The Master pointed to a narrow, high trail winding upward on a towering mountain, so lofty, ominous, that it terrified me. Down in a green valley I saw a thousand lights, heard gay music and people enjoying gala times, which echoed back to us.

"Come back," they called, "join us. There is nothing else save this."

The Path ahead loomed into misty darkness. Only a faint star glowed far on the mountain top. It appeared to beckon, as though whispering, "Have faith and follow the Guru. The God of your heart will not fail you."

"Pensatia," spoke Master H at my side, "choose now, you must. Each who has gone thus far can go back to the ignorance of the Wheel of Life. Yet, once you put foot on yon mountain trail, none dare, or does, betray the Master or the seeking of the Rose. One follows through, up to the breaking of the inner seals into consciousness in the Light. Even though all appears veiled in misty darkness, danger. Remember, Pensatia, they who obey and follow, letting Love and Faith be their only talisman, then shall God and the Masters protect and lead them safely through hell to the unveiling of Isis at the mountain top. Yet man is free to choose. As one dares, all heaven and nature aid him. What say you, disciple?"

I looked into his eyes of such deep wisdom. Shame was mine, that even for a split second the thought of going back had tempted me. "Disciple," he had said. Surely now, I must and I shall make my pilgrimage to the Rose. Let such be the prayer of all who have entered the Path, to be worthy of discipleship.

Then it was I bore upward with my Master, leaving all temporal things behind. A soft wind, rose scented, spiralled down from the starry heights. It seemed to make our footsteps lighter, seemed to bear a song of hope. Angelic beings, a rustling of wings was felt.

"Ah," spoke the Master at my side as we rounded a bend on the mountain ravine, "see, already the Cosmic Hosts bless us, as they do all who seek to pierce ingnorance with the Golden Dawn."

A peace and happiness prevailed within me, even while sadness lay heavy also upon my heart. Oh, to bear with us, loved ones and those who know not there is a Path.

On through nights, days, months we traveled ever towards illumination. Yet always did I bear in mind that all learned on the Wisdom Path had to be given back to earth, nature, and man. The journey was seemingly apart, only as a means to a glorious end: service to God and humanity.

"Always, at this stage, the student trails upwards alone and apart from wordly activities. Though liquidating karma and performing objective duties, one's inner steps seem to be isolated from the crowd. Ever it is so. The nearer the heights, most lonely and barren the Path appears, at intervals, to be. Austere is the scenery. Often only faith in knowing that beyond all obstacles shines the Garden of the Gods, immaculate wisdom, cosmic consciousness supreme. Yes, through the arduous discipline, loss, sorrow of the Way, glows at last the Holy Grail.

"Pensatia, there comes a growing peace, love, power to bless, heal, to serve gracefully each step upon the Path. Let us (each) persevere, know and remember, all who obey the mandamus of the Rose of Life are cared for; even when all supply seems not, the Lord will not forsake thee. Dig thy ditches. Ask, and it shall be; even when you have not, know you *have*. Often the disciple is ready to give up. Only the light and promise of the Masters gives one strength to go on. Thus, little by little, they gain the unfolding of the Rose within.

"Oh, yes, Pensatia, the night will pass. The glorious gold of the inner temple shall compensate for all hardships, opposition, and the letting go of mundane dross. So, when in dire need, be not afraid, for all belongs to the Lord. According to cause and effect, past and present, plus thy efforts to gain the mountain top—so will thy earthly wants be cared for. Yes, even abundance shall be thine.

"Now, behold with thine inner eye."

I did place my consciousness deep within the Eye of

Shiva. So did the Master with his Staff of Azùl, the Staff
of the Hidden One, speak the Word.

Then it was I perceived the crucibles. They were varied.
Different flames of color prevailed. A subtle fire seemed to
burn and mix with the toil and efforts of the aspiring neophytes. Every crucible seemed apart from the others, yet a
rosy beam linked all together with a six pointed star high
in cosmic heaven.

"Yes, Pensatia," spoke the Master, "all trials, labors of
humanity, are one in God's heart. Each bears the inner
signature of the Hexagon."

Everywhere I beheld disciples, neophytes and uncon-
scious workers on the Path. All hammering with the inner
tools, the Golden Key, within their crucibles. Some sang
with uplifted eyes and heart, working bravely to find the
living Rose and Elixir. Steadily, through the purifying
fires they worked. Others stayed in the flames only for a
second, half-heartedly they applied the Sacred Powder to
the crucibles. The transmutation seemed too arduous, too
slow. They fell away into the alluring outer life. Only at
pleasing intervals did they seek the crucibles. At the first
lick of the flames they depart. These bar themselves from
Cosmic Consciousness, for infallible Cosmic Mandate
states, "All must brave the crucibles to win the Rose."
Every step away from the crucibles weakens one's efforts
until all stamina departs. Yet all will have a chance in some
future incarnation to seek the Holy rites. God and the
Masters ever bless these weak ones, for once they too were
weak in some life. They know all will eventually become
Alchemists in the flames of the crucibles. There only gold
is made, and won.

"Ah, look upon the blessed over there. White-haired,
aged, withstanding in the crucibles, even when all dreams
seem futile, when love, home, money, are swept away.
Watch these patient, steady ones. Into the night, the black
and ebony night they toil in the burning fires of transmu-

tation."

There in the alchemist shop I did look, saw old men, women, bent, and etched with sorrow, pain—yet upon their faces beamed a hidden peace, a smile of mystery unexplainable, only by the Holy Grail.

Suddenly a rose mist, a dew, arose within their crucibles and they brought forth a shining key of pure gold, and even as they did, age left them. The marks of their toil, the fire of the crucibles went out; only a luminous white light covered them. They walked forth victorious with the Elixir and the Rose. They *knew*, they *gave*, they *served*, henceforth, each an Alchemist in full regalia and power—the Word, become a living force.

"So must each and all stand within the mystic crucibles and win. No Master, God, or human, can conceive the Key of Life for one. You, she or he alone, only, can bear or build this Esoteric Key to the Immortal Rose. There is no way, except through the alchemist shop, through the fire of transmutation. God, the Masters, all nature aids, protects, guides, at given points. But faith and obedience and one's efforts in the crucibles, alone bring victory. Never seek to escape man's divine destiny. For though eons may pass, all will, must, in some incarnation, face the inner crucibles of the Philosopher's Stone.

"Remember, you who brave the storm, the dark, hunger, torment, the seemingly empty results—stay on. Know, when you least expect, gold will come forth, for use, service and love.

"Yes, Pensatia, it is inevitable that from the Holy crucibles comes Life, Love, wealth and health beyond one's dreams. Yet, remember, when all is given, share it with nature and man; horde it not, even for a day, thy gold, else it will vanish and be no more."

Now did Master H shut off the vision of the crucibles; shut off, he did, our journey.

"Go back and bathe more in the duality of Maya. Yet

keep in thy heart the essence of what is given thee. Until we journey again I bid you farewell."

I turned to speak. The Master was gone. I did obey and did mix in the hustle of earth, and behold, it seemed only a golden part of the whole.

chapter ☆☆ **THREE**

Now, after absorbing and giving back to earth what was received and learned upon my esoteric journey, again I traveled within and up to greet the Master H. And he did take me to a cool, pine scented mountain top overlooking a green valley. A waterfall trickled from the rocks.

Behold, Jesus the Avatar, stood tall, serene, against the background.

"Sit, and listen," my Master spoke.

I obeyed, and Jesus, the Christed One, did bless me, saying, "Pensatia, heed my words. Write from this vantage point."

An angel tall did stand guard, and rose fragrance filled the air.

"This is my retreat. Here I live and breathe the air of the Absolute. Here the winds from cosmic garden blow over me and upon my feet. Here the heart-fire of the Word flows through me and down to earth vibrations. Here I listen, hear and answer all heart prayers spoken with faith. Here I counsel, prophesy and heal. Always my heart is open to the least of humanity. I ever long that consciously man find his way here.

"Speak, Pensatia, ask now, and it will be. Yet ask for others too, else thy asking be in vain. Ask not for temporal things first, but for grace, wisdom, health, love, for, without these all else is empty."

From the depths I asked, and behold a star flashed forth a rosy glow.

"Yes," was whispered on the cosmic breeze, "for all who ask."

"Fear not, Pensatia, and all who reach me here, doubt not, for all that is asked here *will be*. Let not dismay enter thy heart if delays appear. For the answer often arrives over a dark road, and when a great heaviness catches the heart. Realize that when one has asked the harvest is, only the objectivity seems slow."

Now purple tints filled the air on the mountain top. Up from the green valley below toiled a neophyte. With valiant heart he trudged the rugged Path upward. Only the Rose and Lotus guided his steps onward.

"Often from here," spoke the Avatar Jesus, "I flash my image. Love, a word is given, a thought sent, to aid when they obey the Path. Their Teacher and Guru I send to them when they have prepared themselves. Never is the seeker of the Way left to bear his cross alone. The Father is ever with him. In every initiation to high degree the Cosmic steps forth and lifts one across the Astral stream into the pure ether of the White Brotherhood. Only when one disobeys cosmic law and order of the discipline, or *forces* his way through the veil, is there danger.

"Watch, Pensatia, see the potential disciple ever approaching nearer his divine destiny and sanctuary."

Far down upon the Path winding up to Pilgrim's Rest, the weary traveler toiled ever upward. Invisible, perhaps, yet ever at his side a Master walked, watched and strengthened his efforts. Now and then he caught a tangible glimpse, and he bore upward with renewed faith and love. Even though all earthly wealth, home, and mundane joys seemed gone. A star ever beckoned and a voice within whispered that all would be returned at the mountain top.

"Yes, Pensatia, keep faith. Here where I stand serene

beneath the pines of Allah, the Himalayas, far from earth
strife, lies the answer to all who seek the Holy Grail. Remember, within the cup of sorrow is also the cup of joy."

What peace, what comfort, these words from the mountain top. Oh, to stay on the heights, away from earth
strife, sorrow.

"Alas!" spoke my Guru, seeing my unspoken thought,
"only the Masters may abide here. Yet, the disciple, if
faithful, in obedience to the Path, may reach this Shangri-
La in meditation and soul projection. If their desire is pure
and their mission can be furthered by coming here, physi-
cally, in body, or, if certain powers are to be needed in
one's work, then, if karma permits, the way is opened for
a stay in flesh with one's Guru. This is by grace, not by
will of the student. Yet all must travel by soul flight and
know by the awakened third eye the atmosphere of the
Master. One must, through the heart, bathe in cosmic waters and sit at the feet of Jesus and learn what is his cosmic role. Here great healings take place. Here Jesus hears
and lays his blessing of health and plenty upon all who ask
in faith. Never does man ask in vain. If No is the answer,
by law of compensation transcendent strength is given to
bear, and always, if one does not rebel, a victory and cosmic blessing comes and in time the very No turns into Yes.
So, despair not; all who ask here beneath the pines of the
Himalayas receive. If all seems not, give thanks—know,
when least expected aid will come—love, healing."

"Why, beloved Master H, even though one knows the
truth of here, yet when back to earth vibrations, often, it
is as if all were a dream?"

"Have faith, Pensatia. Remember all that is told above
will be below. Seek not the time. Be at peace within. Be
ever patient. Suddenly a new door opens, supply comes,
health blooms, regeneration takes place—outwardly. It
must be if thy Master and Jesus have so spoken. Nature,
all the elements must obey, protect the trusted disciple.

Ask from the throat center, stand in the Golden Flame, drink of the white water of Azùl, and that which is asked will come forth."

A peace beyond compare fell over me like a beneficent mist. We were caught up in cosmic splendor. It was as if body and mind were transmuted into white light of infinite knowing and fulfillment. The song of the spheres poured through my being. I knew without a doubt all travail, all paths lead finally to this Holy mountain top where Jesus stands with open arms to welcome the weary Pilgrim of the Path. If one has found the way here while in the body, death cannot close the door. When transition comes the disciple finds death is just a clearer consciousness of his realization while on earth. To sup with the Masters is the goal of the Mystic Way.

Now, upon the mountain, beneath the pine of Allah, Jesus the Avatar did offer us most Holy bread and wine. Even as we did partake a mystic fusion took place. We knew we were sipping of the Holy Grail. We arose as knighted disciples with cordelia blue and golden staff. Yet, through the lowered vibrations the ageless song of the spheres echoed back from cosmic dimensions and the candle of the Rose of Life glowed warm within our hearts.

chapter ☆ **F O U R**

Again, with the Master, we raised our consciousness to the pine of the Himalayas. There we beheld a circle of disciples sitting on the cosmic green of grass. Tall stood the Master, silhouetted against the Golden Flame of Life. Every disciple received a smile, a blessing.

Turning to us he bade us enter the circle.

"To all here I will give a word that is needed to bring forth for them the Rose of Life."

We opened our inner ears to receive the cosmic lesson. The Christed One did walk the rounds of the circle of twelve. All received.

"Arise now. Obey that which was told thee."

I arose, filled anew with realization of divine blessings.

Now we walked away into the mountain fastness, into a remote glen. Sinking upon the grassy earth I wept for myself and all humanity. Nature, the wee ones, all the plant and animal life worshipped with me and cried out for the ignorance of man.

Now, in solitude I stayed away from the Blessed Ones, from the Master Jesus and the Guru H. I needed to ponder upon all my experiences. Health, wealth, love and perfect self-expression was not, as yet, objectified. In my heart, faith told me the infallible law—as above, so below —would bring forth. In one Holy moment I realized, defeat, loss, illness, all crosses transcended and transmuted into the everlasting Rose of Life.

Yes, all nature bore witness with me to the regenerating waters of life, as they flowed by with silver sparkle and power personified. Into the whirling waters, alone, in naked soul consciousness I bathed in its vibrational current. "Be still," as the Master had taught me, I whispered to the rushing waters. Like a placid mirror they were still. Laying my body upon the earth I did dip my lips and drank, and behold the image of the Christus did appear upon the waters. A voice sounded from the depths: "As you behold my image in all things so shall Love bless, sustain and feed you. The Christus is the infallible mark of cosmic consciousness, the golden stamp of truth. The Christus realized by Krishna, Buddha, Zoroaster, Jesus. It is the divinity shining deep within the heart of man. Only when the disciple becomes aware of the Light within himself, can he sense it in others. To become 'aware of the

Light' is the goal of the Path. All waters of heaven and earth hold my immortal flame. All elements drink from my heart, the Holy Grail. Only the Resurrected Christ can roll away the stone guarding the Rose of Life. Through Maya man walks within to find his immortal self. Only by obedience to the ancient Path of the Masters, by childlike faith, can the Holy Grail be won. In the sunset of the pilgrimage, when mundane shadows whisper of the silence of the evening hour, often, comes the pinnacle of illumination. Not often in the virgin steps of the neophyte, but at the seemingly 'last mile', it is then, if the disciple's heart still dares the upward climb that suddenly a great dawn rises from the hush of the storm, the trials. A curtain is lifted and behold one *knows* all which preceded cosmic awareness, is illusion, self-created. One realizes Light, Life and Love has always been his to claim."

Now the voice did echo as though from a vast distance, yet it was soft and clear within my ear.

"Peace Profound, Pensatia. Ever behold the Red of Rose from Holy Cross."

Drops like woman's tears fell like heavy rain upon me, there in the heights of Ra. A vibrant current stirred my being, sensitizing all my centers. The outstretched arms of the Christed Jesus did seem to gather all life from earth close to his heart. The Word, cosmic music of the spheres, lifted upon infinite realms a mighty crescendo.

Again, Master H calmly stood at my side and cover me he did with golden cape, counseling thusly: "Fear not to penetrate the strata of the Gods, leave all behind, save thy complement in man."

Now upon the altitude of Rose and Lotus a wondrous sight was seen—the fusion of man and woman into the immortality of Love. Saw I earth and heaven as one. Saw the miracle of birth. Golden light from the wedding of the stars. All heaven bore me up to my Bridegroom, for the last words spoken were, "I am yours and you are mine and we both are one in the Lord."

Before the Beloved voice had faded away I was again on earth soil. Master H had vanished. Yet on mundane air lingered a scent of lotus fragrance. A bird sang in nearby tree, as if in song to say, "I too have witnessed Holy sights."

Now a new steadiness centered in my living. I felt purified and ready to travel on with my Guru. All earth work took on a brilliant aura. Everything was a happy task. I thought, how gracious the Word, the Divine Plan. What a privilege the Path of the Rose! Every cosmic dimension earned must be lowered in service to humanity, must be lowered so that worm, leaf, waves of sea, are one with the disciple. What is gleaned above, must be repeated on earth. Love is the blood circulation of God's heartbeat, and so it must flow through humanity.

Ever in our midst, though invisible to the masses, move the White Brethren, those of the White Lodge and Golden Dawn. Yet in ignorance man cleaves to earth only and thus passes by the romance, the Path of Elixir and everlasting life. Yes, within our hearts is that Upper Room.

When night came, and sleep, a joy caressed my soul. Tomorrow, with the first break of day, I would again travel upward with my Guru.

So closes the fourth chapter.

chapter ☆☆ FIVE

Much sorrow has come to me—I who seek the bright summit of the Path. I who would see my Master face to face and feel the golden dew upon my body, have slipt. For a moment the Rose was forgotten. Earth illusion seemed all. And, as always, when one knows the law and keeps it not, the effect was great in price. But as the prodigal son I ran in tears to my Father's house. Behold, from afar He saw and welcomed me, forgiving the stumble, and did say, "All that the Father hath is thine." In white and purple was I gowned, and upon my heart was placed everlasting love.

Again on the Path, sadder yet wiser, I pressed forward to illumination. And behold the God of all people did give me supply, running over for my journey. And Master H did come and say to me, "To all who slip, all is forgiven. Thou art whole. Remember I too, aye, all the Masters on the upward climb, even as you, have fallen from grace. But always they arose and did tighten their cordelias, and, forgiven, they climbed anew to Azùl, to the White Brethren, to the Christus of the Holy Grail."

Now the Master did lead me to a rose garden, among green trees and grass. A clear stream ran through.

"Relax," said he, "drink in the fragrance of the rose."

Obeying, I sat upon the soft waving grass. Great trees shaded us from a sun brighter than any light of earth. Lilies floated by on the running stream. Birds sang. We were indeed in some heavenly paradise. The Master sat near me, and did thusly speak:

"Remember, Pensatia, a thousand times one may negate the Way, yet, if truly repentant, all is forgiven and one starts again upon the Path. The Father understands all earth cares and will fulfill the heart's own needs. So rejoice and drink this Elixir and rose wine. Its delicate pink essence will renew and give one strength to follow the Light."

Reaching out with grateful heart I did sip of the Master's liquid. Gentle peace and soothing filled my heart. Old pains were gone. Old debts wiped out. Gold was in my pocket, my pure desires came alive to meet me. I knew indeed God is Love and Life everlasting and that all is One.

"Pensatia, when you go back to earth vibrations, take

the rose Elixir with you and sip three times three, until thy
body wields the strength of Isis, and even so of earth. Soon
a gate opens for thee, it wends through earth roads and
riches, yet within, its source is born. Heed not what others
tell thee, obey and write of the Rose of Life. Thy words
will live and light the valley for Pilgrims of the Mystic
Way.

"All is given, remember, O readers of the Rose, when
all seems taken away. All is attraction, vibration and
awareness. Have faith and absorb the law. The Word will
break forth. Always the lesser envies what it doesn't understand. Those who dare to stand in the Golden Flame
are above the law of the sweat of the brow. Those who
know this, be humble, give thanks and share thy bounty
as it falls on thee. For they who know the Father's heart,
all is health, wealth, love, and perfect self-expression.

"Remember, Pensatia," came the Master's words, "within, and without ever speaks the Word. Know, on earth
must heaven harvest be. As one lives in super consciousness, so will all materialize on earth. Heed not old wive's
tales or racial negations. Know the law of Life is Abundance. No Master was ever poor. Only through the discipline and karmic night does duality and lack seem. When
we emerge into the Light of soul awareness we attract what
we need. We have access any time to the Father's bounty.
So now let us travel onward to the inevitable summit of
cosmic awareness."

The Master took my hand.

"Come. We toil with joy the upward way. Kindle thy
heart's candle. Be not afraid."

Within the center of my heart I placed my consciousness. Then it was a door opened. We did find the Holy
Grove of green on the mystic Isle of Samos. An amber
light softened the atmosphere. Everything had a clean
fresh tang. A feeling, rather than a seeing, of a vast ocean
surrounding us. A fusion of the elements seemed to take

place, a foursquare union of earth, air, fire and water. We were indeed in a new dimension. It was as though the very essence of Life flowed as cosmic electricity through our bodies, rejuvenating, illuminating.

"Here," spoke Master H, "in this sacred Grove of Samos the disciple rests. One's wounds of travail are healed. He views the crags yet to climb. Under these tall green trees the comfort of cosmic truth is felt, walking hand in hand with nature.

"In the peace of Samos, with the Master one grows sturdy for the climb again. Often a great pain, weariness, penance, sears the heart before the door opens, leading to this occult grove of tranquility. Here all are measured in their cosmic value. The reality back of earth vibrations is shown and taught the disciple. Here the pure spirit of the Holy Grail is revealed by the Christus. One realizes earth and nature are reflectors of the Word. Only man has distorted the vibrational coil of matter. The disciple must learn to synthesize all points of the Triangle into the Hexagon, then Solomon's Seal will shine forth in all its glory. Often many lives pass before one reaches this Isle of Samos, in its green splendor within the Heart's Flame. Here the Rose and Lotus become an objective reality. One learns the poise, the steadiness of eternal signatures. Here as never before the Master stands in the shadows, watching, aiding with cosmic law the disciple to free himself from his karmic dregs, enabling him to cross into the Light of the Mountain Top. It is a beneficent grace and blessing well earned which crowns the disciple now. Consciously, or sometimes in slumber one absorbs higher teachings of the Masters. One, if fitted, is given lessons, experiences needed to bring him into his work or mission. Before one leaves this Grove, one knows his Holy orders and is ready to obey and do. A physical rejuvenation also takes place. It is good to be conscious, objectively conscious, while here; yet, often, one arrives here only in his soul body. Either way, a great initiation is enacted here on the Isle of Samos. Here the Master aids the disciple to gain strength needed for all his outer and inner forces."

Yes, it was true. Night and day I tarried here with my Guru. Earth life became sweeter. Blood and body circulated more life. Heard the Master ever saying, "Obey. All will be." Saw the Star of Heaven beckoning me to follow. Yes, how Holy the Path! Its ruggedness, pain and sorrow, now was transmuted into Gold. All that seemed gone, now came back, for the cosmic reality was seen. Yes, as I obey and write this book, The Rose of Life, each day is blest. God cares for me and ever I feel akin to everything.

So ends the fifth chapter.

chapter ☆☆ SIX

Now the Master bade me arise and face the East and the rising sun.

"Behold," he pointed, "the Flame of Life beyond."

Even as he spoke I felt the Golden Essence of Life flow through the sun disc and all my heart was aglow for the love of the Rose.

"Stand ever in the Gold. No harm or lack can touch they who, even though things seem not, stay in the Golden Flame. Ask what ye will, it shall come to pass, if it be the Father's will. Here, what is thought, positive or negative, is objectified. Very few earn the right to draw the Sun Dew upon themselves. Yet, all walking the mystic Path must attain the Elixir behind the sun. When once attaining the Flame of Gold walk not out of it, for it is life, and more abundant life. As one stands, sleeps and walks in it rejuvenation slowly and surely takes place, and power on all points of the Triangle. Yes, high beyond the sun disc flows pure the Word from God. Here the Holy Ghost, the Dove, flows out to all ready, in sublime initiation. It is only through the Golden Flame that the Stone and fabled Elixir is attained. Herein is all the physical refined and transmuted into one's body of Light.

"So, Pilgrims of the Rose, give not up when thou standest in the Flame and yet darkness prevails. Know O valiant student, blessed and Holy is thy travail. Thy Master, aye, all the Cosmic Hierarchy stand therein, watching, aiding, sweeping aside at climactic periods, all the illusions of Maya and stress of negative karma. This happens only through grace of God and the Master.

"The disciple knows not the exact time his cross will lift. Only know, there is a time when all that has been denied the disciple now comes forth—money, health, love, and one's holy orders. Yes, come it will, the harvest. Yet, often before, there is dearth, hunger, loneliness, often illness. Death seems near. Yet remember this, Pilgrim of the Rose, no matter how old biologically, those who stand in the Flame of Gold *will be rejuvenated*, have wealth, love, and their mission revealed. Their complement in affinity shall come forth, aye, and the two shall wed. Even though past ties prevail and separation by land or sea—two souls meant to meet will, at the epochal moment, be united on the Path.

"Yes, when all seems not, know it is. All debts will be liquidated. All appearances of illness leave. Even now I give to all who obey the drink of Gold itself. Drink three times a day. Drink and speak the Word from the Heart. Sip long or drink at once, it matters not. This drink is most potent to bring forth. When drinking say, or right after, 'It shall be now in the name of Jesus the Christ, not my will but Thine O Father. Let power to do, to give, to love; let health, wealth and my divine mission now come forth.' Then be at ease, and feel the Flame, the Drink doing its Holy work."

O wondrous grace, O wondrous words of the Master, spoken on Isle of Samos. I drink, sip, and speak. Behold I know we live and find the Rose in the center of our hearts. *There* is the Elixir and Stone.

Now the Master H did point upon the cosmic horizon.

"Behold the vast expanse of Akasha. Thereupon is etched the Alpha and Omega of all that is or will be. Look and see your future, which is also your past and present."

Obeying, all seemed black, then misty symbols, pictures, formed upon the cosmic screen. My heart read with ease. My third eye quickened. The glory of the Rose blazed forth. Akasha unveiled past cause and effect and pictured forth the harvest of the Golden Dawn. Yes, there on Samos and up the spiraled Path we came to the leavening heights of the All. Here, beast, plant, earth and heaven and man were seen in their vibrational signature. Here the numbers of all were written. The great organ of the Gods pealed forth. Turning to Master H my soul spoke in silence to him.

"Blessed Guru, God of my Heart, blessed Mary, angelic hosts, give me true vision, true hearing, that I may pen The Rose of Life."

I heard my Master speak.

"Pensatia, it is written in Akasha. Behold, and read."

I turned my eyes upward. Aye, The Rose of Life, all the blessed mysteries given me, were seen finished and brought forth for all to read who would.

The Master laid his hand of power and comfort upon my head. All the Love of the Christus poured upon me.

"Pensatia, all is not in vain. Obey, for when God's time is ripe, the harvest is—my work. Then you, my amanuensis, shall live. My Light shall vitalize all you pen. Obey and write, my witness of the fourth dimension and beyond. Now close this chapter, walk to the green valley of earth, but carry back and pen all received."

"Yes, Master, by God's grace I shall."

chapter ☆☆ SEVEN

The Rose of Life! What a challenge!

The Master came, saying, "Pensatia, consciously or otherwise, East, West, North, South: to the Wisdom Path, to the Rose of Life.

"Come, let us journey now that narrow Path leading straight up to the immortal cosmic light. There is no turning back at this stage, only forward, upward, within. Now it may seem one is thrown back into the snarling arena of Maya. It looks impossible to climb this narrow pathway to the stars and Elixir and the Garden of the Rose. All that precedes this last lap of the journey seems futile, even the Master a myth. Yes, Pensatia, all earth pulls at the disciple. Heaven seems far away. You gaze up. All is mist, winds and crags. Down in the green earth all is pleasant, familiar. It seems to cry out not to leave the last landmark."

In stern voice the Guru now spoke.

"Free choice now is the student's. As one decides so is written one's tomorrow's. I leave you, Pensatia. If you dare to travel yon narrow pass and seek the Holy ingredient needed we will meet again somewhere around the spiral to the goal."

"Master!" I instinctively called. "Master! Stay!"

Yet he had departed before my thought found voice.

A great darkness and loneliness shrouded the Path. A sickness rolled within my stomach. I felt to flee back. Only a stirring within my heart, a potent memory of my Master's touch, caused me to hesitate. Could I fail the Guru? Give up when he had trod the Path—and won? What matter, save the Rose of Life? Try I would. And in the heavy dark I groped and found the trail.

Little by little I gained ground. Ever the Light of the Rose glowed down and lifted my heart in courage. Nights passed and morning in the valley of the earth came with the seasons. And still I kept to the rugged Path. Often was heard the growls of the beasts of the wild. All the sting of the elements bore down upon me. The heat of the fire of initiation sought to annihilate me. I noticed now a lilting fragrance in the air, an essence of attar of roses, or that subtle scent of lotus, while lofty music inspired my efforts to climb the narrow mountain pass. I had no earthly luggage, food or drink, just my consciousness, my urge to dare, only inner faith that somewhere up the trail my beloved Master would meet me. A shooting star whispered Hope. Suddenly a great sickness came upon me—a weariness. I lay upon the mountain trail, that rough terrain so sacred to the Pilgrims of the Rose. A soft touch covered me with warmth. I fell asleep, knowing in waking new strength would gird me to follow through. In my slumber my Guru spoke.

"Fear not, disciple, that which you need will come. Let go of all. Fear not the dour moments, the lonely hours, empty pockets. Keep on, steady, patient, loving and forgiving. Your pockets will be running over when least expected. Give thanks if only for a piece of bread, lo, it will blossom into plenty. In all darkness sleep, work, smile, for the Rose and Golden Dawn must come for all who persevere."

So upon the Path came a new day, came the brightness of fourth dimensional horizon, came the White Horseman over the hills of Shangri-La, came he fast, yet tarrying for a moment. He gave me a look, a beckon. I knew it was a token, a blessing, that all was well there in the "awaking." . . . There in the new day I did arise and taste of the green of nature, list to the bird of heaven, to the music of the spheres. Light as thistledown I arose and did make steps within and without to the mountain of illumination. Joy profound did race through my being as I climbed.

Far down in the valley of earth a cry of lament echoed up to me, a cry of great hunger, making me realize all that is received within must be shared with humanity. Traveling upward time seemed not. Duality left me. The paradox of life leveled into oneness for the first time. Perception of near and far, deep and high was revealed as a whole. In relativity a vision was seen of the end in view. Pilgrim's Rest wafted winds of welcome. In patience and wonder I took each step. And the grace of God did lead me.

Again snow came, spring melted the ice-filled waters, summer warmed the Path, autumn lay naked the trees. Then it was, in the hush of the evening hour the Master came.

"Pensatia," he spoke, "as promised we meet. Not by chance, but by thy well earned efforts—and to all who reach this vantage point, henceforth know, I will stand in the fire of the Holy Grail and behold each step until you make your Mountain Top. Remember, even if appearances are illness, poverty; or even if death seems near, or if forsaken, and the Dark Night rolls over you, you will come through and regeneration will be."

Peace, confidence, walked with me with the Master's presence. Truly, all promises of the Guru are kept. What matter the Cross, Gethsemane, the dregs of Karma? I would follow through. Silence would be my power, my key to the citadel of initiation within the Heart of the Rose of Life. I turned to thank the Master. Lo, he was gone. Yet on the cosmic mind a rose pen flashed these words: "Forgive, love, Pensatia. All needs and measure running over will be thine, and to all who obey."

Flowers, most holy white, of delicate sweetness, fell in showers upon the Path. In the midst I beheld Jesus carrying his Cross up Golgotha's hill.

"Even so, Pensatia," echoed the words, "must all carry theirs likewise."

Now as this seventh chapter closes I sense the Master from afar, sipping from the Holy Grail. There in the pines of the Himalayas, standing close to the Nazarene. There

at the table of our Lord, he did take sacrament with the
twelve. A voice echoed back these words:

"Thus shall all disciples do in time."

Yes, the Path brings one to the mountain of the Gods
and to the communion with their Lord. All who brave the
ascent through the pass and bear the Cross, find here
Resurrection on all points of the Triangle.

O Holy moment! to know the shining Drink, to realize
the Elixir and fabled Stone! Even in sensing the vision,
still, the Path was far up yet. So mote it be we all endure
to pluck the Rose.

chapter ☆☆ EIGHT

Now a synthesis of the Way was built into blood and
bone. One felt a lifting of any physical weakness. Felt
power born of inward light carrying one closer to the Rose
—illuminated. And ever the Master's presence was felt
as he watched from afar. It was beautiful—regenerating—
the Path, now. All nature was green, fresh with heavenly
winds. Humanity touched my heart at every step. Birds,
flowers, even the weeds of wild gardens, seemed to speak
a common tongue. Burdens, lack, were gone. Only the yellow gold Path of the Rose and Cross called me with its
infinite romance—every aspect of earth. The darkest night
was now bright with my consciousness of the inner Light
and auras of everything of earth. All people, Life, was
luminous. The harvest of the long discipline and crucibles
was coming forth. Tears of joy fell as in humble grateful-
ness I gave thanks to God and the Masters for the Love
bestowed upon all who tread in obedience the Way. Now,
in relativity, thoughts became objectified. I longed for

water, and lo, my feet found a spring wherefrom to drink.
When hunger came it was satisfied. The truth dawned of
that esoteric saying of the Christ, "Seek ye first the kingdom of God, and his righteousness; and all these things
shall be added unto you."* And, "Behold, the kingdom
of God is within you."†

"Yes," echoed the voice of my beloved Guru, "as one
becomes integrated in cosmic law he becomes the law,
thus his *words* create. All now is seen in the Holy essence
of the fourth dimension—the Inner Signature. No longer
does the world or outer causes affect the disciple. Where
before he moved by faith only now he *knows* and in knowing has the *power to dare and do.* As the disciple handles
this wisdom and uses it for humanity, so does he ever near
the mountain of Mastership.

"At this stage the vibrations are high. One sees and
feels beyond and above mortal ken. Yet, ever down in the
valley of the unawakened, the Light must be lowered to
serve, and to speak the common tongue. Often one must
forego the right to have, and partake of the lowly stables,
that others might find the Path. Incognito one becomes.
That is, he takes on the garment of those he walks among.
Yet always, Pensatia, mark well these words: *ever within*
he wears the *Mantle* of the *Initiate,* the *Disciple,* the
Adept, invisible save to those of *like evolvement.* They go
forth as directed, and where, to fulfill their cosmic mission.
When God, the Lords of Karma, sound the gong, the
Word is sounded forth for the obedient disciple and one
is lifted into wealth, travel and love, according to one's
destiny. Often now, to the masses, or the unawakened,
one is accused of wasting time. One seems to be doing
nothing of value. Yet, mark well, Pensatia, *if one obeys
as inwardly inspired,* be it menial or creative, or 'just
living,' so does nature and the Master's feed, clothe and

*Matthew: 6:33
†Luke: 17:21

protect. It may appear that I falsify. Yet, disciples, always out of the blue comes thy needs fulfilled."

Even as the Master spoke I sang within, for I knew all these blessed books given me would be published and go forth into the wide wide world.

With new zest my pen was dipped in fourth dimensional well. Yes, now the Path became more luminous. Strength and inner power registered within me at every step. It was as if a higher food, vitamins and minerals of infinite chemistry and vibrational value became supplement to my physical nourishment. I worried no more about supply, for always the Father opened the way. Assurance was mine that all I needed would come. All that mattered was to continue up the spiral to Pilgrim's Rest. What matter the years? I knew regeneration and the illuminated heart would come to every student of the Way when the sacred chakras opened.

Now, in traveling, even a spring burst forth, or Rose Dew sprayed over and through me from above, refreshing, impregnating cells, glands, blood vessels with the rejuvenating fluid of the Elixir.

It was noted the higher one aspires, the more was lifted earth elements, as if all was included in cosmic embrace. Ever was sensed the oneness of the All. Green of earth, blue and gold of heaven fused into glowing whiteness. A polarization equalized, manifested now at every step of the climb to the citadel of Ra, the Lotus and the Rose. Yet, even now, being aware of the clear sweet virility of the Path—even though darkness cleared, I realized there was so much yet to learn, so much to dare—before the Rose came forth triumphant.

The hard climb was not finished. True, my feet were secure on the jagged rocks. Yet, far above, the Star of the Magi glowed like a distant comet. Even so, in my heart I knew the reality was there. So, as a child, let one obey and follow through.

Now upon the Path came She, a woman Master, who, at intervals, comes to all disciples upon the mystic Path. Most beautiful was she. Dark haired and dark eyed and vibrant with woman's love. Tarrying for a moment, her voice spoke out to me.

"Pensatia, long ago my presence was made known to you. Never have you forgotten. Nor I. Now again I come to say: Fear not. All trials will pass. Health, wealth, love, and one's cosmic and mundane expression will now come forth. If it were not so my presence could not be now. To all I come when the time is ripe, and the need is great, nearing yon mountain top. And when the awareness of the Rose Bloom is felt. I come, speak, give to each what they have earned. What I say comes quickly.

"Pensatia, listen, and lay within thy heart my words, for *they will be.*"

I listened and treasured all her message, knowing even as she spoke so would it be.

Only when the Ma and Ra are united, relatively, in the disciple, can the woman Master come. She equalizes the harvest and brings quick results. Men and women both have the feminine Master. Only when the inner is about to be objectified, does she show herself. When she does appear what is spoken will be.

So upon the Wisdom Path, Cosmic words, etched alive upon my consciousness from Akasha's Library, I read: "All evolvement and progress runs in cycles, day, night, seasons. There is an appointed time for everything. A time for the woman Master to appear. A time for harvest. An ebb tide and a flood tide. Appreciate with reverence, both, and usurp neither's purpose. To do so is to deviate from the goal. Bear watching thy esoteric stars, for therein is read the sounding of the gong."

Now the woman Master came up to me, tarrying a momentous moment, saying,

"Pilgrims of the Way, and Pensatia, it will seem I speak

falsely or that I am a fantasy, and my words of worthless value. Doubt not. In faith know. You shall realize that which I have spoken. Nothing in time of finite holds my vision. From above come my words. So let not faith waver. Maya would seek to destroy my presence, my prophecy for each. Heed not. Dedicated now one must be. And obedience to all given is doubly required.

"I leave now. Behold all, the miracle of thy abundance. Give thanks that all is and climb high to yon bright star. Get heaven first and earth responds. Get earth first and heaven is lost. Meet the two in one and you are in the Master's realm.

"Farewell, Pensatia, and like-students of the Way. When my image flashes upon your heart know I am near. Ever will I aid, protect and ease your mundane road."

Smiling, she turned and departed high into the mist of the Rose Dew.

I felt a blessed glow where she had stood. Felt destiny was there, self-made, yet ever glorious when attained. Kneeling upon the grassy ledge leading up, and one with pilgrims everywhere, thanks rose to God for His grace and wondrous laws. And as with patriarchs of old, an altar was built, made of all ingredients found on the Rose Path. Dedicated it was to all who would pass this way. All pain, joy, tears were transmuted into one dewdrop of the Rose immortal.

After prayer I made ready to journey on, knowing those who found my altar would abide therein. So, in time, is built the Pyramid of the Rose. In God's time and man's efforts the Apex will be added, proclaiming the Cosmic Man come forth. O sweet was the essence from the altar high on the mountain pass, and higher, even, the vibrations as I traveled onward. And ever greater was the flow back to earth. Round and round I climbed the dangerous, narrow Path to the luminous Star of Light. Nearer and nearer came the golden breath of Ra. Now, herbs, flowers, their aroma, birds of rare and wondrous color, came upon my vision. And the song of the spheres rang throughout the Path. Small and steady were my feet. All the air of the Rose Dawn spiralled through me, washing one clean, in preparation for the great initiation high in the garden of vision.

Now people of wisdom, those of art, philosophy, science, letters, music, crossed my path. It was as if I made friends of all thinkers, past and present. It was most natural and congenial. I was treated as one in thought and goal. Their inspiration was a benediction. Yet in their exalted companionship I never lost kinship with those in the valley. In fact I felt more closely related, felt their hopes, sorrows, their chains of Maya. Love, compassion and a happy unity was mine now as I traveled the high ascent. Peaceful, easy-like, more stabilizing, earth and heaven fused—as one neared the top. All must fuse in equal balance, for, at the climactic initiation, all of earth we must lay, Christed, on the Altar of the Rose.

chapter ☆ **N I N E**

Now I perceived in my mind's eye and awakened centers a new and Holy gate leading to the White Brethren. Tall, forbidding, they stood guard before the Temple of the Rose. Knowing one must enter to dare further, I made to open the massive doors, but was brought to a quick halt. I felt myself a neophyte. A lamenting tore at my heart. Had I come thus far only to fail?

"God," I made plea, "lead me now to thy sacred Altar, that the bloom of the Rose be known. May we break through the ignorance of our exteriors and open these doors to the esoteric Hierarchy."

Long fell tears. Heavy my pain. Time seemed eternity, and still the doors were closed. Austere, the White Brethren silently flanked the entrance, making no sign of hearing my plea.

"Yes," spoke from afar Master H, the beloved Guru of my journey, "as one ascends to Isis' Sanctuary and the White Lodge, when near the infinite doors of Akasha, naked one stands before the divine portal, realizing in one fell swoop of awareness, the gap between them and the Hierarchal Host. Before admittance, equal polarity of finite and infinite must be ingrained on their credentials. No weakling, anemic student will pass to the exalted Initiation of the White Lodge. Many, reaching this entrance, abide life after life here, building their balance of polarity. For all which is not equalized must be, before these doors open. Soul, mind and body must become one unit. As above so below, as below so above, is the key. Never will the White Brethren and Angels three, guarding the Portal, open, until in degree, the disciple stands foursquare with earth, air, fire and water, fused in blood and bone with their body of Light.

"The cosmic edict is, heaven and earth, man and woman together must enter the spiral within these doors to the Garden of the Illuminati."

I turned, feeling admittance was refused, for, in aloneness I stood. My Alchemy Mate was not. Yet, even in making ready to leave, a flute bore music to my ears. Nearer it came, and with it came "he", wedded in triune affinity with me. As we greeted the wonder of the heavens rolled over us.

Behold, the great doors opened. Hand in hand we entered the spiraled Path to the Rose in bloom.

"Thus," spoke Master H, "must all, man and woman together pass through these doors. Thus must all duality meet and fuse as one before the Elixir and the Stone give passage to the Citadel of Wisdom.

"Yes, at the ripe moment of self-made destiny, when the sacred centers open, the Flute Call resounds far up from out the Mountain of Allah. And behold, the man and woman fated to the Alchemical and mundane marriage, must and will henceforth walk together to the Garden of Vision and the Resurrected Rose."

Now, as we traveled upward, a transcendent fire, gentle, yet enduring, strong, flowed through our being. Consciousness of complete oneness with my Beloved was mine. No words were spoken, yet our thoughts were one living flame. Nothing was hidden. We knew the goal of our meeting was the exalted Third Degree of the Rose, high on the Illuminated Mountain. There we would have the choice of our work, mission, Holy orders, et cetera. We knew all ascetics, hermits, monks, priests, in some lifetime must meet and wed their Alchemical Mate, thus giving birth to the Holy Grail.

"All who negate, or bow to fads, or continuous vegetarianism, or think to gain spirituality in denial will never gain entrance here or meet fulfillment. The middle way is cosmic law—right use of heaven and earth. As one thinks, so is he, truth infallible. The earth is not God but His footstool. Food is not the way to God, but God is the way to food. (Behold a paradox.) All is blest by the pure in heart. All is created in the divine image. *Hold to that in all things*, else walking the Path is in vain."

Now the White Brethren did hand us a bright green capsule.

"This is the cosmic leavener. All must partake who seek higher dimensions and live. Before space is mastered and travel to planets beyond earth becomes possible, man must discover this green essence—within, as well as outwardly, otherwise never can they reach Mars or Venus in earth body. One must earn this inner essence. By this capsule green the greater mysteries of air will be mastered by man."

As we tasted the capsule—it was more an absorption, and quickened our awareness of both mundane and infinite—a gong rang out. "Proceed, disciples of the Way. Yes, even as in nature, green is essential. So here one must eat of the emerald hue. One not ready for the higher green and who dares to sip this esoteric food will only be destroyed. Yet to the true and tested disciple it is beneficent, as is nature when loved. This capsule is green that one may know they are integrated and ready to go on. Otherwise you both would disintegrate before you made another step forward to yon white mountain.

"Behold now the Mountain of Life."

We looked upon a mountain so lofty and white, it drew us like a mighty magnet, yet our exhilaration was steady, healing, peaceful. There was a Path going straight up. Yet with ease we climbed or seemed to float, so light our steps.

Thus man and woman aspired together the ageless Path of Cosmic Consciousness. Color, song, wondrous scenery stretched from both sides of the Path. Angel wings flanked our boundaries, as though showering blessings. A fragrance, rose sweet, traveled with us. We were conscious of other like affinities climbing upward with us. Love pervaded the air. Far and high on lofty summit the Christus looked down. His compassionate eyes bade us come and sup with Him.

Continuing upward my Beloved's thoughts were one with mine.

Oh, that all could reach, attain the Alchemy Marriage! Bear the crucible, oh neophytes. Faint not, for yonder is the mountain all seek. It rises white within thy heart. Seek the Path, oh reader, again within thyself, to at last find the white mountain here. Pray God we all attain the Holy Grail.

Suddenly darkness shrouded the white light of the summit. A heavy fog made dark the Path. Holding to my Beloved's hand tears fell, pain came, where before joy had prevailed. All seemed fantasy.

"Come, let us return," I cried, "we have been duped."

Then we saw far down on earth people vivid and happy, heard their laughter.

"Look, it's there we should be, not here."

"Silence," spoke he, my love. "Know you not, faith has brought us thus far, and faith will penetrate this darkness. At every high step one must pass through a dark night. Let us persevere, as we have, in the long travail of the Path. This is only our challenge to another dimension of Attainment."

"No, no," I answered. "It is enough. Go back I must."

"You shall not," answered my mate. "Wielded in cosmic rites, together we go forward. Fear not, Pensatia, this too will pass. Suffer not this mirage to delusion us."

His words brought comfort to my heart. I was ashamed of my weakness.

"Chide not yourself," he spoke, reading my thought. "All grow weary as the summit nears. Let us lift up our voice in praise and thanks. Let us go on joyfully through this moment of night."

Even as we did, soon we perceived a beam of white light flowing from the mountain top, guiding us through the dense fog.

"See, Pensatia, what faith does? No matter, storm or stress, it never fails. Thank God for our blessings."

"Beloved," I spoke, "I realize why man and woman are fated to travel yon mountain together. May I give to you in some crisis as you have given to me."

He smiled. "You have, Pensatia, even though, often in the beginning it seemed unrecognized. It is written, 'Those of fated polarities give from cosmic garden one to the other, even if one or the other, objectively, is unaware of the interchange.' Always here in consciousness they meet and travel to the summit as one. It is called 'journey's end.' Yet we know it is only the beginning of ever higher dimensions of living. The vastness of God's wonder can only be learned by degrees."

Now the atmosphere again took on a rosy hue, and it seemed our bodies assumed and exuded a regenerated glow, as though the Elixir brought new life to organs, cells and glands.

Oh, to bring this experience back to earth! Words are so inadequate. Yet as we receive we must give in some measure.

"Remember," spoke he, my Beloved, "in all earth clay is found the divinity of the All. In nature runs the fiat of all cosmic law. On this sorrowing planet of earth man is initiated into the crucibles of soul alchemy.

"Forget not at the highest the depths from which one climbs, neither those who dwell in the valley."

Walking was bright now. All earth hunger, duality, was gone. We were nearing a far new country of cosmic vibrations. Our mind was clear with Soul Light. All was seen in relationship to the whole.

chapter ☆☆ **TEN**

Out into the ether. Up to the eternal quest.

I asked, "Is this what happens when death releases the soul?"

From the Master came the answer. "Yes, when one has attained cosmic consciousness in life, death is only the same, free of the physical, or the lifting of the body into its transmuted essence. If the interior senses remain unawakened, in death one is bound by such limitations, though certain progress is possible, if the desire to learn is zealous. Even so, the greatest growth comes in earth incarnations. The fiat from the Word is: Cosmic Illumination must be attained while on earth. All must find in some life the Path within and endure the crucibles. Gold, the Elixir, the Stone, must be made on the loam of earth."

It was becoming cold as we traveled upward. We now experienced a freezing barrier blocking our way. It was as if guardians of the Light were placing a mighty challenge, as though all hell and the Black Brotherhood of all negation, in guise of a raging blizzard, dared us to go further. I drew close to my Beloved. We bore through the storm which beat us to our naked skin. Stumbling we groped our way.

"Master, Master," we cried out together. No answer, only cold wind, icy silence. A numbness passed over our bodies. Only a faint glow far up shone upon us. Only faith kept our courage. An intangible strength kept us climbing "Roseward," to the heights. With the cold came quick night on the mountain pass. No longer could we see or feel the Path beneath our feet.

"We're lost!"

"No," spoke he, my Beloved, "God and the Masters still are with us, even though it seems not."

His words warmed my heart as an inner fire.

"Look," he said, pointing through the dark cold.

A light came from an open window high on the mountain bend. It seemed to bear an invitation. A rustic veranda overhung the rocks, giving an extensive view of a green valley. Just a glimpse, then blizzard winds and snow obliterated all.

"Yes," spoke my mate, "it is the resting house of Pilgrims on the Path, of which we both have heard. We must make it, Pensatia, and, by God's grace, we will, for there we must tarry, to rest and prepare for the ultimate journey to the Mount of Initiation."

Holding my hand within the strength of his own, we felt, rather than saw the Master's presence, touch, guiding us safely through the dark. Suddenly the cold and snowy winds ceased. We stood at the door of the wayside house. There, on the way to the Shangri-La of soul consciousness, we gave a prayer of gratitude and did knock. The door opened. Behold, my Guru stood, broad shouldered, gray of hair, his massive beard blowing in the now soft, mellow air. Balmy breezes floated up from the valley below.

"Come in, and welcome, valiant disciples of the Rose," greeted us the Master H, his gnarled staff held strong within his hand.

Within a fire burned bright on a massive rock hearth. A broad, long table, Gothic, faced windows overlooking the green valley. A tall chair was placed at the middle facing the East. There the Guru sat. We sat on a bench, opposite the Master. We awaited his words. All wounds of the storm had vanished. Peace Profound filled the room.

"Let us eat first," smiled the Guru.

Even as he spoke, fresh green salad graced the board, meat and wine of clear sparkle.

"Eat hearty, disciples."

Surely, we thought, God supplies all needs, often in mysterious ways.

The Master sensed our wonder and made answer.

"To they who know the laws, nothing is a miracle. Yet, seek not the how or why now. Hunger must be satisfied and God provides, even at the last moment."

The food was good and rejuvenating, and quickly refreshed us. The wine had an esoteric flavor, or so it seemed. The Guru did partake also, though with moderation. We felt the power and healing vibrations of his aura, positive and radiant with his love and light. Just to sit in his presence was as a benediction. We felt the Christus overshadowing him. Yet he was most human and natural. Inner strength was revealed in every action and word. Amber light filled the room. Pleasant winds came softly through the window. A wild rose climbed up and peeked with green leaves into the room. Its fragrance lingered about the Master's aura, who then arose.

"Come, disciples, let me show you to your rooms."

Obeying we were given adjoining quarters, facing the veranda, revealing the sweep of the mountain top. We marvelled at the up-to-date conveniences—showers, lights, et cetera. The Master again smiled.

"If one knows the laws, all can be given for man's comfort, anywhere at any time; yet the lesser must be Christed before the Word obeys."

In rich simplicity the rooms were furnished. Soft greys, blue, with touch of canary yellow, was the color effect. In each room stood a flat-topped desk with mirror overhead, before which was placed a large comfortable chair. On the desk was candle and incense of sandalwood burning. A single fresh rose graced a small blue vase, embellished with Egyptian symbols. A single bed and bureau, early American, completed the furnishings with rare white throw rugs upon grey floors. All spotlessly clean.

We turned to thank the Guru.

He spoke. "Here Pilgrims of the Rose and Lotus, rest, renew themselves, meditate and gather strength to make yon high mountain," he pointed out the window. "By your own efforts you have reached this esoteric wayside house. Only those who obey and keep on the Path—in spite of all odds—attain here. Some in soul projection, or in dreams, a few in flesh, yet that is rare. Still, if one's mission is aided by coming thusly, God and the Master will make it possible. The lessons needed will be given you. Each will study alone. Even so, what is learned must flow one to the other and hence out and down to earth. . . ."

Now days went by. Nights and a myriad stars shone over the wayside house high on the mountain pass.

We renewed ourselves in the rarefied mountain air, acclimated our bodies to the alchemical challenge of the mountain top. We meditated within the heart's altar and wisdom from the Holy Grail was bestowed upon us. We toiled with new faith there in the wayside house and knew we were nearing the secret of making Gold and the fabled Stone. We knew when again we resumed the upward climb the pinnacle of the Rose would be ours in all its glory. In infinite dimensions we would receive our Holy orders. To know the privilege, glory and obligations presented there on yon mountain top would be indeed Life, Light and Love. Yet, even though we were affinities on all planes of consciousness, we realized Holy orders might again separate us bodily. We felt, however, that before this obtained, the choice would be ours to make.

Anticipating we knew not what, we sipped of the cup of happiness at this oasis of fulfillment, granted us during days spent in this haven in the remote Himalayas. Yes, that grand passion immortal of soul we experienced. And the wild rose climbing from the window sill, the soft valley winds bearing upward, seemed to bless our transcendent love. We knew the final rites, the Rose Wedding, would be consummated when we attained the Star of Isis on the Mount of Illumination.

Then one evening, when the cycle was ripe and the cosmic gong sounded, and the Lords of Karma spoke, the Guru, the noble Master H, called us to the massive long table in the room where we first had entered.

"Sit," he requested, "I would talk with you.

"Beloved disciples, in faithful study and happiness you have deported yourselves with infinite credit here. Now the time is ripe. Depart in peace and with new steadiness and inner strength attain Cosmic Illumination. And may the apex of the Rose indeed bloom for you. Here I watch, knowing all that happens. If you stumble, arise, and boldly climb. At yon mountain top you choose the glori-

ous Third Degree, or the lesser, yet both are acceptable
to the White Brotherhood and the God of all."

"So be it," we arose and spoke as one. And the ancient
mystical Rosy Cross on golden cord was placed about our
necks.

"Take nothing on this journey save your consciousness.
Naked, gowned only with your heart's light and the Robe
of the Initiates."

Even as he spoke we found ourselves out on the Path
ascending on high. Though we were stript of all earthly
garments we were not without apparel. It was fine, luminous, and of golden color. Weightless, these garments
seemed to blend and fuse with our whole beings. God and
the Masters, the very stars of heaven seemed to bear us
upward.

How blessed, we thought, God's Love. How beautiful!

Now the vista ahead—all nature—made way for us.
Though steep the Way now, a star of gold shone bright
upon us from the mountain top. It was as if God, the
Angels, and the Masters made preparation for our welcome. Distant flute music rolled down from the Pinnacle
of the Illuminati. My hand lay warm within the comfort of
my Beloved.

"Pensatia," he spoke, "no greater love than this, to
travel upward, to Peace Profound."

"Yes," I answered with my heart, "great indeed is the
grand passion immortal between man and woman."

Now night came, and on the hearth of Cosmic Path we
slept in soft and gentle slumber. And Master H did come,
in the silence of the night, flowing inner strength upon our
interiors, that when daybreak should awaken us, regeneration would gird our pilgrimage.

And through the night old songs and loves of earth
crept up and through our dreams, and cuddled close, as
if to say,

"All is *one*."

chapter ✭ **ELEVEN**

Morning broke fresh upon the narrowing of the Way.
We arose, fortified with the Rose essence of Dew, and did
drink from the flask of nature as it brewed the secret
potion of Ra Ma into our veins.

And now upon the Path came the hoary ones, the
Venerables, the vanguard and custodians of the Way.
They marched on either side, while swirling waters and
thunder of darkness, the lightning, the dark currents and
storm, all came to no avail against the phalanx of the
White Brotherhood, protecting us upon the dangerous
heights of Cosmic Consciousness. They neither spoke nor
looked our way—the Hierarchal Masters—but straight
they walked, as if to lead the Way. Even as we pondered,
Master H's voice spoke directly, close within our ear.

"Give thanks, disciples, for, if the wall of Masters
infallible did not protect the Bridge ahead no disciples
could cross. For there the Black duality, the negative 'left
hand' adepts apply all their arts and cunning to pull back
the Pilgrims of the Holy Grail. But all who reach here,
beyond the Wayside House, have earned the protection
and service of the Masters. Have no fear, Beloved Ones,
climb on, you will win and cross the Bridge—to Cosmic
Consciousness."

Now, a sense of awe, an awareness of some stupendous
occasion facing us ahead warmed our hearts. We heeded
not the wild and subtle attacks of the Black Adepts. Even
when we came upon sylvan meadows drenched with heavy
sweetness of lush red and purple flowers, with sinister black
clouds hovering overhead, drowsy music calling us to rest,
intuition bade us keep on. We found our steps hard to
take. Our thinking seemed dense. I felt my senses slipping
away. Had it not been for the firm touch of my Beloved's
hand upon mine, I would surely have sunk into the subtle
allurement of psychic phenomena. Yet with every step

victorious we gathered new strength, confidence.

Softly came Master H's voice through the cosmic mist.

"Never accede to the allurements of the Path. Never sleep in the in-between phenomena, else the Hierarchal Rose can never bloom for thee."

Now the Path led straight up, high and narrow. Single file now, we trod the ascent. In the near distance a White Bridge loomed. The one we were to cross. Silence reigned. Like a profound jury, we felt all depended on whether we were able to cross over the link between two worlds. No breeze. No Presence, save the consciousness of our goal— the Illuminated Mountain Top. We came suddenly and fatefully to the swinging Bridge of Light. We steadied our hearts with a plea to God and the Masters. Eternity lived in our consciousness. We stood there on the great divide, knowing if we crossed we would, for a second, know the whole of life, the *meaning* of the Path. All was dark, save the misty white of the crossing. No encouragement came. No music of the spheres. Not even could we see the Star upon the Mountain Top.

Suddenly my Beloved spoke.

"Here we part. Alone we must take this Bridge of Ra. Go in courage, Pensatia. Wait. I will meet you, when I, too, have made passage. If *either of us* lose our step—or senses—and are swept into the psychic abyss below, know we will meet and win in another incarnation. So let us say together, 'Memoria hominum tenear!' 'Let me remembered be!' We felt rather than gave embrace. Then in aloneness I walked the Way to the Mountain Top, walked steadily, strong in faith. The Bridge swung far and near, like unto a mighty earthquake. Earth and Heaven seemed to roll about me.

"Master, Master," I cried.

All my centers broke asunder with cosmic cleavage, and Light—blinding Light broke over me, and a great wind bore me across. I sank on a level of earth, yet, heaven

poured over and through me in White Light, more powerful than a thousand suns, yet the green of earth equalized
my polarity and I lay with a grateful heart, suspended in
cosmic dimensions.

And behold, again I felt the presence of my Beloved, my
complement in Man.

"We made it!" he exclaimed, taking me in rapturous
embrace.

Now, angels came and did bring us drink of the Elixir
and bade us rest there in the impenetrable land of the
Mountain Top. And there in what seemed an oasis of
slumber we sank in rest and the Master, near yet far,
whispered,

"Well done, disciples of the Holy Grail."

We awoke in the dazzling purity and essence of Light,
Life and Love. We stood together in the clarity of the
whole. And God and Hierarchal Masters, the Dove and
Holy Ghost was in us and about us. Our consciousness
was of earth, yet transcended, and was endued with the
living wonder of the Golden Dawn.

We were each adorned with a robe of gold, with purple
cordelia wound about our waists. A star, the Pentagon,
shone from our foreheads, while over our hearts throbbed
in fragrance elusive, violets, drenched in dew of Rose. And
behold, my Mate held a staff within his hand and I a silver
wand, and green buds sprouted all about. We felt alive
with power, and love flowed from our hearts' center down
to mundane vibrations. How profoundly peaceful!

We spoke together our thoughts, and behold, a ring
of gold circled my finger and a voice resounded: "THE
TWO ARE ONE."

Now, a touch, a presence, was felt. A hand upon our
shoulders, and behold Master H, the Guru of the Path,
said:

"Follow and enter the Temple of Citation."

On the Mountain Top all became dark, black, like wing

of raven.

"Fear not. Walk straight ahead. Before every Holy Initiation or blessing one must, by faith, walk in the blackness."

And again the wind howled and all the tempters of the Black Brotherhood sought to grapple with our souls. But with the staff and wand held firmly in our hands, we bore onward, obeying the Master's voice.

"On and up, O valiant ones."

We heard rushing waters on every side. Lightning flashed. Yet, strangely calm, even in joy supreme, we made our way to Temple of Isis Unveiled. Yes, the Rose and Cross stood high at the entrance of Holy Pillars, upholding the Altar of the Rose. And our Guardian Angel led us within where a Shekinah blazed with virginal, everlasting Light.

We knelt and kissed the Cross, "The Old Rugged Cross," and from the center a Rose bloomed and behold —we were transfused and became one with the symbol.

And all Heaven opened, and earth, and all planets, and all nature. And Man was seen in the hollow of a mighty Hand. And a great Eye glowed warm and loving upon all.

And we knew ourselves to be standing in consciousness of The All.

Aeons seemed to pass, and all the "Sweet Mystery of Life," unfolded before us. We knew to ask was to receive. To seek was to find. And Heaven was within.

Then we looked in the distance along a hall, or corridor, with vaulted roof of blue and a million lights. At the end of this lighted corridor we saw a great chair, raised upon a high dais, and the Venerable One, Guardian of the Book of Akasha, sat within.

"Go," the Guru Master H said, "and receive your Holy Orders."

chapter ✩ TWELVE

We stood with hushed reverence before the White
Light of the Mountain Top. A great sadness *and* a great
joy prevailed within our hearts: joy that at last we bore
witness to the Rose of Life: sorrow that all in the valley
of earth were not with us. All the privileges, responsibil-
ities, spoke aloud as a cosmic voice, saying, "All that is
received must be given back. The Rose self-bloomed must
flow its essence back to the valleys of humanity. Such are
the Holy orders of all who seek the shining Holy Grail.
Here in the Garden of Allah, the oath is taken."

The All-Seeing Eye bore upon us and Golden Flame
in spiral form lifted us up to the Throne of Isis. There,
male and female, two souls as one sat resplendent,
crowned with Cosmic Consciousness. The Rose of Life
bloomed triumphant from the heart and head centers,
which met forming golden light from the Eye of Shiva.
The Initiates of the Light arose and walked back to earth
vibrations. Their mission was ingrained upon their heart
centers. And all the stars of heaven smiled upon them.

Master H came walking out from Shangri-La and
thusly spoke:

"You who dare the citadel of the Rose, be seated, and
know your destiny high, where only the pure voice of the
Hierarchy, the blessing of the Holy Ghost is available."

In this nobility of cosmic worth we pondered and
weighed our thoughts. We had earned the presentation of
our "orders." In our Heart's Altar the sacred fire burned
high. Naught of mortal inception could pass this Infinite
Degree. Only truth, hard won, awareness beyond and
above the temporal could make the invisible visible. We
sat, united in our oneness of goal, yet, in our wedded
affinity we knew each to be complete within himself. We
had earned the Love granted us, though now, by choice
—outwardly—we might be parted. We knew ever we

would inwardly commune, one with the other, through distance and space, bound by the law of affinity.

Now came the Venerable Ones, the Guardians of the Rose of Life. Came they with silver key, and a gold and jewelled one with scroll attached.

Each numbered: The Pythagorean Way, the Mystic Seven, the Celestial Twelve, the Karmic Five, and the Three of Expression.

Came He, the White One of the Hidden Rose, came He who watched and waited for Humanity's Initiation, two by two, on the Luminous Mountain Top.

Silence reigned as the blackness beneath the deep sea. Expectancy was king within our senses. Yet a new Peace Profound was ours. We sensed our journey back to earth. All mundane vibrations were seen in true perspective. A glorious service for the God of our Hearts awaited us on our return.

"Yes," I turned and spoke to he, who through the cosmos, by inner signature was my own. "What shall we choose? The earthly mating or that beyond?"

Our Hearts made answer.

"We go back together, yet in another life we will take a still higher Degree into the Rose of Roses."

Tears, like dew of the Path wet my cheeks.

"Master. Master H," my thoughts cried out loud, "without you there is no triumph. Blessed Guru, could I ring out one truth upon the Path to the wide wide world, it would be:

"The Masters *are; seek* and *find*. Obey and brave the crucibles and Gold will be. And the Rose will flower."

En rapport, my Beloved acquiesced.

The Venerable Guardian stood tall, commanding, before us.

"As you choose, so shall it be. Here, you bear witness to the inner signature of the Rose of Life. So, now, down yon Path back to earth. Let your light touch all who pass your way. All earthly *needs will be met*, as you speak *in faith* the Word.

"In this life, by choice, you will not enter into the severance of all your earthly ties. Yet know, to God and the Masters, each path of service is precious in the records. Know, it is to the Disciples, the Adepts, and Devotees, that the New Age looks.

"Here on the Mount of Illumination, the sum total of the Way flowers for each. The Light is stabilized in consciousness within the center of one's being. Here in the Holy stillness one is fortified and given daily 'orders' for one's mission, or soul work.

"Remember, upon achieving this pinnacle of initiation, the Rose of Life is yours to use at will, for the service of humanity."

"We go," we spoke aloud, "within, to the God of our Hearts."

And, arising, making the sign of the Rose and Cross, we did turn our face from the Mountain Top and made ready to descend again to earth vibrations. Yet, within our Hearts we carried Peace Profound, and our Holy Orders. Carried we Love, conceived and born from the crucibles.

Thus it is through Rose and Cross, through the Ageless Way, one finds the Golden Dawn, and knows without a doubt, THERE IS A ROSE OF LIFE.

. . .
. .
.